HERE'S JUGGINS

By Amy Wentworth Stone
Illustrated by Hildegard Woodward

TABLE OF CONTENTS

CHAPTER I

THE SURPRISE

JUGGINS LIVED IN a little fishing village called Blue Harbor, in the littlest house in the village. It had two rooms and four windows and a door and a little green pump in the kitchen where she washed her face and hands every morning. Her real name was Lucy Belle Tibbetts, but her daddy called her Juggins.

Her daddy, big Tom Tibbetts, was a fisherman, and so was Juggins. Behind the house by the road was a board sign, which said:

T. TIBBETTS
FRESH LOBSTERS—LIVE OR BOILED

And under it was nailed a small shingle, reading:

L. B. TIBBETTS
CUNNERS FOR CATS—
NICE FAT SNAILS AND ANGLE WORMS
FOR FISHERMEN

Every summer morning Juggins and Daddy rowed out of the harbor in the big dory to pull their lobster traps, and when it rained, Juggins wore a little sou'wester and a slicker just like Daddy's.

Here is a picture of one of Juggins' lobster traps just after she and Daddy had dropped it over the side of the dory, down to the bottom of the ocean where

the lobsters crawl around. Juggins and Daddy were up in the dory, on top of the water, at the other end of the rope, and they were tying it to a little stick of wood called a lobster buoy, so they would be able to find the trap right away when they came out the next day to pull it up.

There must have been a lot of lobsters in it when they pulled it, for they were beginning to go in through the little round door. Juggins had put a piece of fish inside that smelled very good, and big lobsters, middle-sized lobsters, and baby lobsters all went walking in. They did not know that the little round hole was a trap door and that when they were once inside, they could never get out again until Juggins and Daddy came to open the trap. Juggins always felt sorry for the baby lobsters.

"They are so little," said Juggins. "I don't like to have anybody boil them and eat them up."

So when she helped Daddy take the lobsters out of the traps, Juggins always stood up in the dory and threw the babies back into the water, as far away from the traps as she could.

One morning when Juggins woke up, she remembered, even before she opened her eyes, that something nice was going to happen. On Mondays

after breakfast, she always took lobsters up to Madame
Eliot's big gray cottage on the hill, and Madame Eliot
had told her that the next time she came up with the
lobsters, she would find a surprise waiting for her.
For a whole week Juggins had been thinking about
that surprise and wondering what it could possibly be.
Daddy had had a twinkle in his eye, as if he knew all
about it.

"Is it a real surprise?" said Juggins to Daddy. "Or is
it just a nice, fat banana?"

But Daddy would not say a word.

And now it was Monday morning.

Juggins pushed back her patchwork quilt and sat
up in bed. The little bare room was full of bright
sunshine, and Daddy's bed in the other corner was
empty. He must be getting breakfast now. Juggins
could hear something sizzling on the wood stove
in the kitchen, and there was a jolly smell of fried
cunners all through the little house. Cunners are little
fish that smell ever so good when they are cooking
for breakfast. Juggins peeked over the foot of the bed
into the kitchen. She did not see Daddy, but she saw

something else. The little pans which she and Daddy had put on the floor the night before, under the leaks in the roof, had water in them. It must have rained in the night.

"Oh, goody!" said Juggins.

Sometimes when it rained, the wind blew on one side of the roof, and then the rain came down through the leak at the foot of Daddy's bed; and sometimes it blew the other way, and then the rain came down through the leak at the foot of Juggins' bed. Daddy and Juggins had made up a nice game about this.

Whoever had the most water in their pan after a stormy night might choose any cup in the whole house for breakfast—even the best blue china one on the top shelf. Juggins always chose that one. It had rosebuds around the edge, and she felt like a princess when Daddy poured her milk into it. Juggins liked the leaks in the roof, and she felt sorry when Daddy said that they must work hard at the lobster traps to earn enough money to mend the roof before next winter.

"Don't let's earn *too* much money," said Juggins.

"Don't you want a new dress to wear to school?" said Daddy.

"Oh, yes," said Juggins. She had forgotten that she had only one real dress.

But the leaky roof was fun.

This morning Juggins thought that her pan looked very full. She jumped out of bed in her white cotton nightie and ran to see. Sure enough, the water was up to the brim. Then she went and looked in Daddy's. It was only half full.

"Goody," said Juggins again.

Then she ran into the kitchen to find Daddy, but he

was not there. She looked out between the blue cotton curtains of the back window. She could see the road and the pasture sloping up to the big cottages where the summer people lived. Sometimes Daddy went up very early to Madame Eliot's with mackerel for her breakfast. But there was no one on the hill now.

Then she looked out between the blue cotton curtains of the front window, and there he was, coming up the path from the float, with a pail of something in his hand.

"Hello," called Juggins between the curtains, "I won!"

"Sure you did," said Daddy, setting the pail down under the window. Then Juggins saw that it was full of live lobsters, all green and wiggly.

"I suppose I shall have to go up with the lobsters myself this morning," said Daddy, looking at the white nightie.

"Oh, no," cried Juggins, and she scampered into the bedroom and began to dress as fast as she could. She put on her blue shirt and fisherman's overalls and buckled her sandals. Last of all, she tied a strip of blue cotton around her yellow topknot, to keep it out of her eyes. Then she ran into the kitchen.

She was in such a hurry that she almost forgot to wash her face and hands at the little green pump. When she was all ready, she brought the cornbread and the rosebud cup from the cupboard while Daddy took the cunners, all crisp and brown, from the stove. Then they sat down at the little table and had a very nice breakfast. Juggins had caught the cunners the night before with her own little fish pole and line, so they were very fresh indeed. And the milk was so good in the rosebud cup that Daddy had to fill it three times.

When they had eaten all the breakfast, they went outside and Daddy tied the lobsters together with a piece of string because the pail was too heavy for Juggins to carry up the hill. There were six middle-sized lobsters and one big grandfather lobster. Daddy put wooden plugs between the claws of Grandfather Lobster, to keep him from snapping. Grandfather lobsters have very bad tempers indeed. Juggins could hardly wait for Daddy to tie the last knot.

As soon as the lobsters were ready, she picked up the string and walked off across the grass as fast as she could. She wanted to run, but it was never a good plan to run with lobsters because they bumped against your legs. Juggins had known a great many lobsters, and she was not a bit afraid of them, but they were very snappy, and they did not like dangling on a string.

Juggins walked across the road and up the little path through the pasture. As she went along, she was very happy because she was thinking about the surprise. After a while she saw that the plug had dropped from between one of Grandfather Lobster's claws. It must have caught in one of the bayberry bushes along the path and been pulled out. Juggins put down the lobsters and hunted all around in the bayberry and sweet fern for the plug, but she could not find it. So she picked up the lobsters and started on again. But now she had to walk more slowly because she had to hold Grandfather Lobster's snappy claw away from her legs. It seemed a long way to Madame Eliot's this morning, and Juggins began to be afraid that she would be too late for the surprise.

At last the big gray cottage among the spruce trees came in sight, and in a minute Juggins was knocking at the kitchen door. She knocked and knocked and knocked, but nobody came. Perhaps, thought Juggins, Katie, the maid, was giving Madame Eliot her breakfast on the front porch—she sometimes did that when the sun was bright and the sea was blue. So Juggins put her lobsters on the grass by the doorstep and tiptoed around to the front of the cottage. It seemed to Juggins the biggest house in the world, and it made her want to walk on tiptoe. When she came to the porch, there was Madame Eliot at a little table, sipping her coffee. With her shimmery dress and white hair, she looked to Juggins just like a queen. And there beside her was a plate of nice, fat bananas.

"Good morning, Lucy Belle," said Madame Eliot, smiling down at Juggins. "Are you our lobsterman this morning?"

"Yes'm," said Juggins, at the foot of the steps, her hands behind her.

"And have you seen the surprise yet?" said Madame Eliot.

"I—I don't know," said Juggins, looking out of the corner of her eye at the bananas.

Just then something happened.

There were suddenly shrill screams from the side of the house, and around the corner came a little boy. Juggins had never seen him before, and she wondered how such a thin little boy could possibly make such a loud noise. He was running as if something very bad indeed were behind him. And something was.

"Why, Joey!" cried Madame Eliot, getting quickly up from her chair. "What *is* the matter?"

"Oh, oh, oh!" cried Juggins.

"Granny, Granny, *Granny!*" cried Joey, scrambling up the porch steps, "Takey Toff! *Takey Toff!* TAKEY TOFF!" And he buried his face in Madame Eliot's skirt.

And there, holding fast to the seat of Joey's shorts, was Grandfather Lobster, with all the other lobsters trailing behind on the string!

Juggins scrambled up the steps after Joey and took hold of Grandfather Lobster. Then she pulled and pulled until off he came, with a piece of Joey's shorts tight in his claw.

"Oh, dear," said Juggins, looking at the shorts with a very scared little round face.

As soon as Juggins had taken off Grandfather Lobster, Joey stopped screaming. He felt around behind him with his hand, and when he was sure that there was nothing there but a hole, he lifted his head from Madame Eliot's skirt and looked at Juggins. As soon as he saw her, he began to laugh. She was still holding Grandfather Lobster.

"Hello," said Joey to Juggins, "I'm going to stay here all summer. Can you play with me? I'm the s'prise!"

And Juggins thought that he was a *real* one!

CHAPTER 2

BARNEY'S POCKETS

WHEN KATIE HAD come out on the porch and taken
away the lobsters, Madame Eliot gave Juggins and
Joey each a nice, fat banana. Then she went into the
house. Juggins and Joey sat down on the top step of
the porch and ate their bananas. They peeled them
down very slowly so that they would last a long time.
After a few minutes, Tansy, Madame Eliot's big yellow
cat, came and sat down beside Juggins. Tansy liked
Juggins. He was one of the cats for whom she caught
cunners. Juggins broke off a piece of her banana
and held it to the tip of Tansy's nose, but Tansy just
sniffed and looked the other way.

"I will bring you some fish this afternoon," said
Juggins.

From the top step, they could look off through the little spruce trees at the ocean and the bank of fog offshore. It had been misty in the early morning, so Juggins and Daddy could not go out to their lobster traps, but now half a dozen little white sails were skimming over the clear, blue water.

"I like boats," said Joey. "I've got one."

"So have I," said Juggins. "We've got two."

"Mine's a toy boat," said Joey, "but Granny's going to have a real motorboat. A man is building one for her now. Are yours motorboats?"

"No," said Juggins, with a little sigh, "just a dory and a punt."

Juggins wished every day that motorboats did not cost so much money and that she and Daddy could have one, like the other fishermen. It was hard work pulling the old dory out to the lobster traps when the sea was rough. Daddy said that all Tibbettses were made with fine strong muscles in their arms, just to pull dories with—but whenever she had a wishbone, Juggins wished very hard indeed for a motorboat.

"Will you take me out in your dory sometime?" said

Joey to Juggins.

"Yes," said Juggins, "you can come this morning."

"All right," said Joey, his face all smiles. And he got up from the step and hurried to finish his banana. "Where shall we go?"

"After lobsters," said Juggins.

"Oh, no," said Joey, sitting down on the steps again, the smiles all gone. Joey did not want to catch any more lobsters.

"You could take your toy boat," said Juggins, "and see if it will really float."

Joey thought about this for a moment.

"Well," he said, "I'll get it." And he ran into the house.

In a few minutes he came out again, wearing a new pair of shorts and carrying the boat.

"What a beauty!" cried Juggins, clasping her hands.

And indeed it was. It was painted white, with a wheel like a real motorboat and a little brass anchor in the middle of a tiny coiled rope on the deck. There was also a little sailor in a white suit and cap standing at the wheel. On the side of the boat was painted its

16

name, the *Squid.* Juggins touched the little sailor's cap and suit with her finger to see if they were made of real cloth, and they were.

"Granny says I may go," said Joey. "Let's start now."

"Yes," said Juggins, and she led the way around the house and down the little path through the pasture. Joey followed close behind, carrying the boat.

When they had gone a little way, they saw a man coming up on the path toward them. As soon as Juggins looked at him, she knew by his squinty, scowly face that he was Jem Bass, the fisherman who lived

by himself over on Back Cover. Juggins was always a little scared when she met Jem Bass because he looked so unpleasant. He was scowling now as he came along up the path, and Juggins and Joey stepped aside into the sweet fern to let him pass.

"Hello," said Juggins, as he strode by. In Blue Harbor, if you were polite, you always said *hello* to everyone, whether you knew him very well or not.

But Jem Bass just grunted and did not even look at Juggins and Joey. Suddenly he stooped and picked up something at the edge of the path. Juggins saw right away that it was the little wooden plug that had dropped out of Grandfather Lobster's claw on the way up the hill.

"Oh," she said, "it's my plug!"

Jem Bass now looked at Juggins. "You Tibbettses mind your own business," he growled, pocketing the plug.

"Oh," said Juggins again, her cheeks very pink. Nobody had ever spoken to her like that.

Joey began to run down the path, but Juggins stood still in the sweet fern, too surprised to move. Jem Bass turned and started up the hill. Then he looked back, and his scowl was blacker than ever.

"And you tell your dad," said Jem Bass, "to keep his hands off my lobster business."

Juggins looked up at him with round eyes.

"My daddy never touched your lobsters," she said sturdily, although her heart was thumping very fast.

Then, frightened, she turned and scampered down the path. Juggins and Joey ran, without looking back, until they came in sight of the road and of Juggins' own little gray house on the rocks. Then, as they stopped for breath, they saw another man coming along the road. But this time Juggins was not a bit scared. It was Barney Williams, the old boat builder from the end of the harbor. Next to Daddy, Barney was Juggins' best friend, and as soon as she saw his stooping shoulders and his old corduroy jacket, she began to run faster than ever. Sometimes Barney carried very nice things for little girls in the great wide pockets of that jacket.

"Barney," cried Juggins, "oh, Barney, wait for us!"

Old Barney looked up and waved his hand. Then he

stood in the middle of the road, his pipe in his mouth.

Juggins came racing down the little path, her arms spread wide, with Joey and the boat at her heels. They came so fast that just at the end of the path, Juggins tripped over a stone, and Joey tripped over Juggins, and down they went, boat and all!

"Hello," said Barney, as he picked Juggins out of one bayberry bush and Joey out of another and the boat out of the sweet fern, "what's all this—a shipwreck?"

When everybody was right-side up again, and Joey had made sure that there was not even a scratch on the boat, Barney patted one of the big pockets of his corduroy jacket.

"It seems as if I felt something in here," said Barney, with a chuckle.

"What?" said Juggins.

Barney held the pocket open, and Juggins put her hand down into it. The pocket was so big that Barney could carry his tools in it, but now all that she could feel was a two-foot rule and a fish line. Then she laughed, for she felt something else.

"Are they from Mrs. Milly Willy?" asked Juggins.

Mrs. Milly Willy was Barney Williams' nice old wife and another of Juggins' special friends.

Barney nodded his head. Then Juggins took her hand out of the pocket, and there was a cookie as big as Barney's hand. The cookie was cut in the shape of a fish, and it was covered thick with sugar.

"Now it's your turn," said Juggins to Joey. "There are some more in there."

So Joey felt around in the big pocket, and when he took out his hand, there was another cookie, cut in the shape of a boat, and *it* was covered thick with sugar too. Juggins and Joey each took a big bite.

"Yum, yum," said Joey.

"What's in the other pocket?" said Juggins, walking around Barney. There was something very bulgy indeed in that pocket.

Barney's little black eyes twinkled, but he would not let anybody look.

"When we get to the house, we will take it out," said Barney.

Juggins touched the pocket on the outside of the jacket.

"Oh, I know!" she said, jumping up and down. "It's somebody for the family. Oh, goody!"

"What?" said Joey.

But Juggins would not tell either.

Then Juggins took hold of one of old Barney's hands, and Joey took hold of the other, and together they dragged him as fast as they could along the road to the little gray house on the rocks.

CHAPTER 3

WHERE IS GERALDINE?

THE BULGY THING in Barney's pocket was a thick stick of wood. It had a funny face painted on it at one end, with a grin and a little sharp wooden nose sticking up in the air. It also had a painted yellow jacket and a ring of rope through its head instead of hair.

"Oh," cried Juggins, as soon as she had pulled it out of Barney's pocket. *He's* handsome!" And she held it out for Joey to see.

But Joey looked disappointed.

"It's only a doll," he said.

"No," said Juggins, "it's a lobster buoy."

Juggins knew all about lobster buoys, for she had a large family of lobster buoy children that Daddy and Barney had made for her. There was Tiny Tim

and Geraldine and Mr. Hoover, and ever so many
others. Nobody had ever given Juggins a real doll,
but the lobster buoy children were much nicer to play
with because they could go swimming with Juggins
in summer and coasting with her in winter, and they
never broke their legs because they hadn't any. They
all had grins and little sharp noses, and they all wore

bright yellow jackets so that Daddy and Juggins could
see them easily, bobbing up and down on the blue
ocean. Juggins' children spent nearly all their time out
at sea tied to the lobster traps. She missed them, but
she saw them every day when she and Daddy went
out to get lobsters, and she let the children take turns
coming ashore to play with her.

"It's Geraldine's turn to come home today," said

Juggins to Barney, "I shall tie the new one to her trap instead. I do want my Geraldine."

Old Barney chuckled and pinched her ear. Then he pinched Joey's.

"You'll soon be a fisherman too," said Barney.

Then he filled his pipe and went off up the road.

Juggins and Joey ran around to the front of the little gray house, and there was Daddy with a pair of oars over his shoulders. It was time to go out to the lobster traps.

"Can Joey come too?" said Juggins.

"Sure," said Daddy.

So they all went down the rocky little path to the float.

There were two boats tied to the float—the little green punt, with the words "Pea Pod" painted on it (that was Juggins' boat), and the big white dory (that was Daddy's). Daddy untied the dory and pulled it in. While he was doing this, Juggins and Joey put the *Squid* into the water. It floated beautifully.

"Let's tie it to the float till we get back," said Juggins. "We can pretend it's waiting for a cargo. Boats do."

"All right," said Joey, although he was not quite sure what a cargo was.

So they uncoiled the tiny rope on the deck of the *Squid* and tied it to an iron ring at the edge of the float. It did look very cunning riding up and down on the harbor waves, just like the *Pea Pod*.

Then Daddy lifted Juggins and Joey into the dory. He put them side by side on the stern seat. It was not a wide seat, and Juggins was a very wide little girl, but Joey was a narrow little boy, so they just fit in with a new lobster buoy child between them. Daddy jumped into the dory and pushed it off. Then, standing in the middle of it with his back to Juggins and Joey, he began to row down the harbor with long, smooth strokes.

The sky and ocean were a jolly blue, and there was sunshine everywhere, although out beyond the harbor, Juggins could see a long dark streak of fog against the sky. Side by side on the stern seat, Juggins and Joey sniffed the fresh salt breeze that was blowing in from the sea and were very happy. After a while they came to Mad Cap Island at the mouth of the harbor. There

they met a motorboat coming in. A tall old fisherman was standing up in the motorboat, and as he went by the dory, he put his hands up to his mouth and shouted to Daddy.

"Hi, Tom!" he called. "They've seen that red robber out there again this morning, but they lost him. He went into the fog again."

Daddy stopped rowing for a moment.

"Were the traps touched?" he shouted back.

The fisherman was already too far away to answer, but he nodded his head.

"Oh, dear!" said Juggins. She had heard Daddy and

Barney talking only yesterday about the dreadful things that were happening out at the lobster traps.

"Who's the Red Robber?" asked Joey, sitting up very straight. "I love robbers."

"But he's not a nice robber," said Juggins. "He steals lobsters right out of people's traps."

"Why don't they catch him?" asked Joey.

"They can't," said Juggins, "because he only comes when there's fog, and he hides in it, and he wears a red scarf up to his ears, so nobody can see who he is. Oh, I hope he hasn't taken our lobsters."

"I wish we could see him," said Joey.

Juggins stood up in the dory and looked out to sea at the Red Robber's hiding place.

"Perhaps he'll come out of the fog," she said. "We can watch now, and whoever sees anything can say, 'Oh.'"

So Juggins and Joey sat on the edge of their seat and watched the fog bank with round eyes, while Daddy rowed the dory out past Mad Cap Island into the open ocean, straight toward the Red Robber.

Suddenly Joey said, "OH!" very loudly indeed.

"You haven't seen anything," said Juggins, looking all around.

But Joey had—only it was not the Red Robber. It was an ocean swell, and to Joey, who had never been out on the ocean before, it looked as if a mountain were coming right down on him. The other end of the dory began to go up and up, and in a moment he and Juggins were sitting on top of the mountain; then down they slid into a blue-green valley—and there was another swell racing toward them.

"I think we'd better go home now," said Joey, in a very small voice.

But Juggins laughed.

"It's fun," she said. "It's like coasting." And after they had gone safely over two or three more of the big swells, Joey began to laugh and think it was fun too.

Every time the dory went up to the top of a swell, Juggins and Joey looked off across the sea for the Red Robber, but nothing at all came out of the fog. Soon there began to be little bright yellow spots on the swells. They were Juggins' lobster buoy children, bobbing up and down in the sunshine. Daddy pulled the dory up beside one of them and stopped rowing. Juggins leaned over the side of the dory and looked.

"It's Mr. Hoover," she said, patting him. "He needs a new grin."

Daddy leaned over too and pulled Mr. Hoover and his rope, and out of the ocean and over the side of the dory came a big lobster trap, dripping with seaweed. While Daddy emptied a great many wiggling lobsters out of the trap, Juggins stood up in the middle of the dory, her feet wide apart, and held the oars. Juggins was a good little fisherman and never lost her balance, even when they went over some very big swells

indeed. When the trap was empty and Juggins had thrown the baby lobsters as far away as she could, she put a piece of fish into the trap for bait, and Daddy dropped the trap and Mr. Hoover back into the water.

"I think the next is Geraldine's," said Juggins, and she leaned over the side of the dory to look for her favorite child.

But the next trap was Tiny Tim's, and the next was somebody else's, and as they went on over the swells and there was no Geraldine to be seen, Juggins began to be very sober indeed.

"Maybe she was dragged in the storm last night," said Daddy. "We'll find her farther on."

But although they rowed back and forth and emptied all their traps, there was no sign of Geraldine anywhere on the ocean.

"Oh, *dear!*" said Juggins, and she looked down at the lobsters in the bottom of the dory because she did not want Joey to see two big tears.

"That's a fine catch," said Daddy cheerfully, looking down at the lobsters too. "I guess the Red Robber hasn't touched our traps. If you can sell those lobsters, maybe you can be spending money for something."

"For a motorboat?" said Juggins, blinking at the lobsters.

"No," said Daddy, smiling at Juggins, "but maybe a zipper jacket."

"Oh, goody," said Juggins, looking up again and smiling too.

Juggins' old sweater had five holes in it, and she did *so* want something that zipped.

But as soon as Juggins looked up, she caught her breath, for there was the fog close in her face. While they had been hunting for Geraldine, it had come silently in.

"Oh, hurry Daddy," cried Juggins. Like all good fishermen, she had been born with a fear of the fog.

But Daddy had seen it too and had picked up the oars and begun to row as hard as he could for the harbor. The gray curtain of mist was just behind them, and little wisps of it were already flying over their heads.

"The Red Robber!" said Joey, looking over his shoulder. "Perhaps he's chasing us in the fog."

"Yes," said Juggins, and she looked back too, but she

was more afraid of the fog than of the Red Robber.

Juggins and Joey sat very close together, with the new lobster buoy child still between them. Once when Juggins looked back, she thought that she saw just the tip of a boat peeking out of the mist, but it was gone right away. Then all at once, a boat did come out of the fog, close beside them. There was a flash of red, and both Juggins and Joey squealed and hid their faces in their laps. But when Juggins peeked up out of the corners of her eyes, it was only old Barney in his motorboat. He had been out to his traps, too, and was waving his red handkerchief as he went chugging by!

The dory went on toward the harbor, with the long smooth strokes of Daddy's oars, and soon they were going in past Mad Cap again, with clear water ahead. They had beaten the fog and the Red Robber.

When they had slid safely up to the float and Daddy had lifted Juggins and Joey out of the dory, the first thing they saw was a really truly cargo in the little *Squid.* Somebody had left a fishing line on a reel, with a hook and sinker, for Joey.

"It's Barney," said Juggins. "I felt it in his pocket."

"Now I can go fishing too," said Joey, very much pleased.

"We'll go right after our dinners," said Juggins.

Joey picked up his boat and the fishing line and started up the rocky little path. He wanted to have his dinner as soon as he could. Halfway up the path, he looked back.

Juggins stood in the middle of the float and smiled at Joey, but she was not quite happy. She was thinking about Geraldine and wishing that she knew what had become of her. But if Juggins had really known where poor Geraldine was, she probably would not have been happy at all.

CHAPTER 4

CUNNERS FOR CATS

AS SOON AS Juggins had finished her dinner, she took
a small can from the shelf, and a tin spoon, and went
out into the little potato patch behind the house to dig
angleworms. Once a week Daddy liked to go fishing up
at Fresh Pond, and then he needed plenty of worms
for bait. It was a very rocky little potato patch, but
there were lots of angleworms in it.

Juggins got down on her knees among the potato
plants and began to scoop out a small hole in the soft
earth. Very soon two fat brown angleworms came
wiggling out of it. She picked them up and brushed
them nicely and dropped them into the little can. Then
she scooped out another hole.

She was digging away busily and thinking that

Joey must long ago have finished his dinner, when suddenly through the potato plants she saw two slim legs coming along the road close by. They were not Joey's because they wore long, creased trousers and had very large, beautiful sport shoes at the ends of them. Juggins went on scooping in the earth with her spoon until the legs stopped right in front of the

potato patch. Then she sat back on the heels of her sandals and looked up. She saw at once that the legs belonged to the new young man who had come to live in the summer cottage next to Madame Eliot's. He was reading the words on the shingle sign by the road, and he looked like a very pleasant young man indeed. When he had finished reading, he turned to Juggins.

"Are you L.B. Tibbetts?" he asked.

"Yes," said Juggins.

"Well, what's the price of angleworms today?" he inquired.

"They're one cent for fifteen," replied Juggins.

The young man whistled.

"Very nice and fat?" he said.

"Oh, yes," said Juggins. And she held up a fat brown one between her thick little finger and thumb.

"Then," said the young man, "I'll have thirty."

"Oh!" said Juggins. This was a very large order indeed.

The can was already half full, so Juggins tipped the angleworms out of it and began to count.

"Shall I put them in your pocket?" she asked, when she had counted out thirty.

"Well—no," said the young man, "I believe not. They might come out, and it happens that the friend I am going to walk with doesn't care for angleworms— except on a hook. Here, suppose you put them in this."

And he picked up an empty little tin tobacco box that somebody had thrown down by the roadside.

So Juggins packed the angleworms into the tobacco box. It was a tight fit, and the angleworms could not have been at all comfortable, but they all got in somehow.

"I had to put in two thin ones," said Juggins, "but they were extra long."

"That's great," said the young man. And he gave Juggins two shiny pennies and put the box into his pocket. Then he went down the road. He turned at the bend and waved his hand, but Juggins did not see him. She was looking up into the pasture at something that was coming down the little path among the bayberry and sweet fern. It was certainly Joey's head that was bobbing along above the tops of the bushes, but below his head he looked very strange indeed. In a minute he ran out of the path into the road, and Juggins in the potato patch stared harder than ever. Joey had been changed during the dinner hour. He was very fat around the middle and with legs that looked thinner than ever.

"What's that you've got on?" said Juggins, as Joey came up, a little out of breath. She tried hard not to giggle, because she knew that it was not polite to laugh at people, but Joey did look very funny.

"It's a cork jacket," said Joey. "Granny says I have to wear it when I play near the water, so I'll float if I fall in. Are we going fishing now?"

"Yes," said Juggins. "We must catch some cunners for Tansy and for Mrs. Milly Willy's cat."

So Juggins and Joey went around to the front of the little gray house. Two fishing poles were lying on the grass. One of them had a line on it. That was Juggins'. She tied Joey's line to the other and picked up a can of snails from the doorstep. When you go fishing in salt water, you cannot use angleworms. Then Juggins and Joey ran down the rocky little path to the float. Juggins put one of the snails on Joey's hook and one on hers. Then she showed Joey how to throw his line into the water. They stood side by side at the edge, and Joey did just what Juggins did.

All at once Joey began to jump up and down on the edge of the float.

"Oh! Oh!" he squealed. "Something's got hold of my line! They're pulling it away! Oh, oh, oh!" And Joey held onto his pole with both hands and capered about in his cork jacket until Juggins was sure that he would fall into the water.

"You've got a *bite!*" cried Juggins, as soon as she could stop laughing. And she took hold of his pole and jerked it up into the air—and there on Joey's hook was a fine big cunner. Joey was very proud and pleased when he saw that he had really caught a fish. Juggins took the cunner off for him and put another snail on his hook, and they went on fishing. Very soon Juggins caught a cunner, and then Joey had another bite, but this time he did not jump around or squeal. He jerked the line into the air, just the way Juggins did, and landed his own cunner right in the middle of the float.

They fished until they had each caught four cunners, and Juggins said that was enough for today. So they lifted their lines out of the water and turned to pick up the fish. Then they stared very hard at the float, for there was not a cunner to be seen! But there was a flapping of wings overhead.

"The gulls!" cried Juggins.

And when they looked up in the air, sure enough, there was the tail of their last fish dangling from the beak of a large gull.

"Oh, oh!" cried Joey in despair.

"Never mind," said Juggins. "We can catch two more. That will be one for each cat."

So they threw their lines into the water again, and very soon they each had a bite.

"They're the biggest ones of all," said Juggins, as she took the fish off the hooks.

She put her cunner in one of the breast pockets of her overalls, and she put Joey's cunner in the other, because his pocket was covered up by the cork jacket. Juggins thought that the cunners looked very large and fine with their heads sticking out. She and Joey left their fishing poles by the doorstep. Then they started along the road toward Mrs. Milly Willy's. Barney and Mrs. Milly Willy kept the little store at the end of the harbor.

"We can see your Granny's motorboat," said Juggins. "Barney's building it, and it's grand." Juggins sighed a little, as she always did when she thought of motorboats.

The road wound along by the edge of the harbor, past ever so many fishermen's cottages. They were all bigger than Juggins' little gray house, and in

the biggest of all lived Amos Alley, the constable.
Constable was what they called the policeman in Blue
Harbor. Every day Amos Alley sat on his side porch in
his shirt sleeves and watched people going by on the
road. And once in a while, he took somebody off to
jail. He was sitting on the porch today, very thin and
solemn, as Juggins and Joey went walking by. When
he saw Joey's cork jacket and the heads of the cunners
sticking out of Juggins' pockets, he leaned forward in
his chair and stared at them over his spectacles.

Juggins and Joey walked as fast as they could, and
when they came to the bend in the road, they began to
run and never stopped until they had run up the steps
of Barney's little store and were safely inside. Mrs.
Milly Willy, plump and cheerful, in a pink cotton dress,
was sitting behind the counter making a hooked rug.

"Well, bless my soul!" said Mrs. Milly. "What's all this?"

"We've got fish for Muffin," said Juggins. Muffin
was Mrs. Milly Willy's cat.

"Fine!" said Mrs. Milly Willy. "And Muffin has
something for you too."

"What?" said Joey.

Just then Muffin herself came in at the door and ran behind the counter.

"Is it what you said you'd give me the next time you had any?" said Juggins.

"Sure," said Mrs. Milly Willy, looking merrily over her spectacles.

"Oh, goody," said Juggins, and she ran behind the counter too.

CHAPTER 5

JUGGINS SELLS THE LOBSTERS

BEHIND THE COUNTER at Mrs. Milly Willy's feet was
a box of hay, and in it were Muffin and two tiny fluffy
gray kittens.

"Oh, Mrs. Milly Willy," cried Juggins, "which can I
have?"

"Whichever you want," said Mrs. Milly Willy.

Juggins picked up one of the fluff balls very
carefully by the back of its neck, and Joey picked up
the other.

"I'll have this one, with the black nose," said Juggins.
"Can I take it home now?"

Juggins had wanted a kitten for a very long time.

"Well," said Mrs. Milly Willy, "I think if I were you,
I'd wait until it likes cunners."

Juggins took a cunner out of her pocket and held it
to the little black nose.

"Oh, dear," she said after a minute, "I guess I'll have
to wait for a pretty long time."

So she and Joey put the kittens back into the box,
and she gave the cunner to Muffin, who liked it right
away and ran off with it behind a flour barrel.

There were ever so many barrels and boxes
around Mrs. Milly Willy's store. There were shelves
too, full of cans and packages of things to eat, and
more shelves full of cotton cloth and ribbons and
fishermen's gloves. There was even a glass case on

the counter, with gumdrops and licorice and chocolate mice in it. It seemed to Juggins that there was everything that anybody could possibly want in Mrs. Milly Willy's store. Best of all, there was a rope high up across the front window, and on it hung a row of jackets that zipped.

Juggins ran across the store and looked up at the jackets. Yesterday Mrs. Milly Willy had let her try on a little blue-and-white check one that was exactly the right size. Juggins had been afraid ever since that somebody else would take it away before she and Daddy could sell enough lobsters to buy it. And now she could not see it at all among the red and green and gray jackets for the big fishermen. Juggins walked back and forth, reaching up to push the jackets apart. Then all at once, she saw a bit of blue.

"There it is!" she cried. "*Do* you think it will wait for me, Mrs. Milly Willy?"

"Sure," said Mrs. Milly Willy very cheerfully.

But Juggins did wish that one didn't have to wait for quite so many things.

Mrs. Milly Willy now opened the glass case and

took out two chocolate mice, one for Juggins and one for Joey because they had brought Muffin the cunner. They were very fine chocolate mice, with pink peppermint eyes and long elastic tails, and they were much too beautiful to eat. But in just a minute there was nothing left of them but the two elastic tails.

"Now let's go and see the boat," said Juggins.

So Juggins and Joey said goodbye to Mrs. Milly Willy and the kittens and ran out of the store and down the grassy slope toward the harbor. They could see the motorboat gleaming white in a little open shed among the fish houses by the edge of the water.

"Barney's painting it," said Juggins. "It's almost finished. Perhaps he'll let us help."

But when they ran into the shed, Barney was not there. The boat was standing, big and high, across some blocks of wood a little way above the floor. When it was quite finished, Barney would push it off the blocks, out through the front of the shed, and down a sort of little runway, like a toboggan slide, into the water. Barney called this launching the boat. Juggins loved launchings, because you never knew

48

whether boats were really going to float until they slid down into the water. She was always excited and a little afraid that they wouldn't, but Barney's always did. Soon she would see this one go sliding down into the harbor too. Juggins stood on tiptoe and peeped over the high curving rim.

"It's wonderful," she said, feeling the smooth wood and sniffing the fresh sprucy smell.

"I'll take you out in it when Granny gets it," said Joey proudly. "I guess we can catch the Red Robber with that boat."

"Yes," said Juggins, "I can see a place for the engine, and it's ever so big."

Joey tried to peep over the rim too, but he couldn't on account of the cork jacket. So he ran around to the other side.

"There's some paint here," said Joey.

Juggins ran to look too, and sure enough, there was a can with two brushes in it. That side of the boat had not been painted at all.

"Let's finish it for Barney," said Juggins. "Now, before he gets back."

So they each took a brush and began to paint as fast as they could, Juggins at one end and Joey at the other. After a while the ends of the boat began to be a beautiful shiny white. So were the tips of their ten fingers and Joey's cork jacket.

"Won't Barney be surprised?" said Juggins.

But it was not Barney who was to be surprised first.

Juggins was painting away at the bottom of the boat when suddenly she heard footsteps on the grass outside. She put her cheek down on the floor and peeked under the boat. But it was not Barney's old fisherman's boots that Juggins saw. Instead, coming along over the grass toward the shed were the very same large beautiful sport shoes that she had seen through the potato plants after dinner. And beside them were walking another pair of beautiful sport shoes, only ever so much smaller. Juggins knew right away that they must belong to the friend who did not care for angleworms except on a hook. Juggins stopped painting and sat as still as a mouse, hidden behind the boat. And so did Joey. The two pairs of shoes walked right into the shed. They must have been trying to find Barney, for this is what Juggins and Joey heard over the top of the boat:

"He's not here, Cherry."

"Oh, Ted, I don't know where else to go. The lobster roast is tomorrow afternoon, and I just won't have Jem Bass's lobsters again. Who else can sell us fifty?"

"*I* can!" said Juggins. And her head popped suddenly over the rim of the boat, like a jack-in-the-box. At almost the same moment, Joey's head popped up over the other end.

"Oh!" said Miss Cherry, with a little squeal.

"Can *what?*" said Mr. Ted, looking down at Juggins.

"Sell you fifty lobsters," said Juggins, looking up at Mr. Ted.

As soon as she looked up, there was a funny little white thing bobbing around in the air in front of her. She squinted at it, and then she saw that it was the end of her nose with a blob of white paint on it. It must have hit the boat on the way up. Joey looked as if his had hit something too.

"Are you painting the boat or each other?" inquired Mr. Ted.

But Miss Cherry smiled at Juggins from under her little pink hat.

"Will you ask your daddy," said Miss Cherry, "to bring fifty lobsters down on the rocks for the lobster roast tomorrow afternoon, and will you and Joey come too, and help us to get the seaweed?"

"Oh, yes'm," said Juggins, with a little jump, and her eyes were very bright over the rim of the boat.

As soon as Mr. Ted and Miss Cherry had gone away up the hill, Juggins ran out of the shed. She could hardly wait to get home to tell Daddy about the lobsters. She forgot the boat and Barney and Mrs. Milly Willy and the kittens. She almost forgot Joey, who panted along the road behind, trying to keep up. And when they came to the little path up through the pasture, and Joey said goodbye, she forgot the cunner for Tansy that was still in her pocket. But as the cunner was white with paint, Tansy probably would not have liked it anyway.

"I've sold the lobsters! I've sold the lobsters!" sang Juggins, as she skipped along the road and around the corner of the little gray house.

And there was Daddy sitting on the doorstep, smoking his pipe, all ready to be told the news. When Juggins had told it, and Daddy had pinched her cheek and wagged his head, as he always did when he was very much pleased, Juggins sat down on the doorstep too.

"Do you s'pose," said Juggins after a minute, looking up out of the corner of her eye, "do you s'pose that fifty lobsters are enough for a zipper jacket?"

"Well—maybe," said Daddy.

Then Juggins was very happy, for when Daddy

So Juggins sat on the doorstep beside Daddy.

said *maybe* like that, pleasant things almost always happened.

So Juggins sat on the doorstep beside Daddy and looked out to sea and thought what a nice day it had been. And it was not until she was all tucked into bed that night under the patchwork quilt, and Daddy had taken away the lamp, that she thought about two things that were not so nice. She remembered that she did not know what had happened to poor Geraldine, and she remembered what Jem Bass had said up in the pasture, about leaving his lobster business alone. Juggins did hope that Jem Bass would not be very cross because she had sold Miss Cherry the lobsters for the lobster roast.

And then she thought of the lobster roast and of all the jolly things that were going to happen tomorrow— and before she had thought of half of them, Juggins was fast asleep under the patchwork quilt.

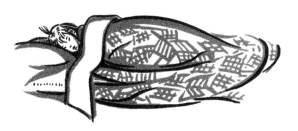

CHAPTER 6

THE LOBSTER ROAST

WHEN JUGGINS WOKE up on the day of the lobster roast, she did not see how she could possibly wait for the afternoon to come. As soon as she had finished her breakfast, she ran to the kitchen shelf and looked up at the clock.

"How many times will the big hand have to go all the way around before we can take the lobsters over to the rocks?" said Juggins to Daddy.

"Nine times," said Daddy, for it was only half past six.

"Oh, dear," said Juggins, staring at the clock, "doesn't it ever go around faster than that?"

"Not while you're looking at it," said Daddy.

So Juggins turned her back on the clock, and

washed the cups and spoons, and polished the little wood stove with a blacking brush. Then she looked up at the clock again.

"Daddy," she called, running to the door, "it's going faster!"

"Sure," said Daddy.

Daddy was mending a fish net in front of the house, so Juggins went out too, where the net was spread on the grass, and hunted all over it for the holes. Juggins liked to help mend nets with Daddy because they played that every time she found a hole, she had caught a fine fish. The big holes were whales, and the little ones were cunners. This morning the net was an old one, and Juggins caught twenty whales. When they had finished, she ran in and looked at the clock again, and it had gone around very fast indeed.

"I guess it *does* like not to be watched," said Juggins. So she did not look at it again for ever so long.

She sat beside Daddy on the doorstep while he spliced a rope. And after that they went out in the dory to get their lobsters. And then they bailed the boats. And then they had dinner. And then—when Juggins at last looked at the clock again, it was after three, and time to get ready for the lobster roast!

She put on some clean blue overalls and scrubbed her face and hands very hard at the little green pump. Then Daddy put the lobsters into two big pails, and they started along the road to the Point.

The Point was a long stretch of flat rocks at the mouth of the harbor, and when the tide was low, as it was this afternoon, it was a beautiful place for a picnic fire. Before Juggins and Daddy had come to the end of the road, they could see a column of blue smoke rising above the little spruce trees, and when Juggins ran ahead and came out upon the cliff, there was a fine bright fire leaping and crackling between two big rocks down on the Point. Mr. Ted and Miss Cherry were throwing driftwood on the fire. Joey was there too, and as soon as he saw Juggins, he waved his hand and came running to meet her.

"I didn't have to wear my cork jacket," said Joey, "because there'll be so many people here to pull me out if I fall in."

Daddy carried the pails over to the fire, and Mr. Ted took some money out of his pocket and handed it to Daddy. It was more money than Juggins had ever before seen all together. Miss Cherry said that the lobsters were fine, and Juggins smiled at Daddy and was very proud and glad.

When Daddy had gone away, Mr. Ted said that it was time to get the seaweed for Miss Cherry. So he and Juggins and Joey ran down to the edge of the ocean, where the seaweed hung, wet and brown, on the rocks. Mr. Ted had on fisherman's boots today, instead of the beautiful new sport shoes, and he stepped right into the water and pulled off handfuls of the seaweed. Then he gave it to Juggins and Joey, and they ran back and forth, carrying it to Miss Cherry by the fire. Miss Cherry piled it on an iron shelf over the fire and buried the lobsters in it to cook. Juggins knew just how good the lobsters would taste steamed in seaweed.

It was fun skipping from one flat rock to the next and jumping over all the little saltwater pools. There was no fog today—just the clear, blue ocean as far out as they could see. Juggins wondered where the Red Robber went when there was no fog. Perhaps he was hiding out there among the green islands beyond the bell buoy. She could see the little black bell buoy rising and falling on the water offshore, and she could hear its faint tinkle. Sometimes, when the sea was rough, and the bell buoy was tossed about on the waves, Juggins could even hear it in the little gray house after she had gone to bed. She liked the sound of the bell buoy because she knew that fishermen out at sea in the dark would hear it, too, and be able to find their way safely into the harbor.

When Juggins and Joey had brought enough seaweed for Miss Cherry, Mr. Ted said that they must have more driftwood for the fire.

"It takes a lot of wood for fifty lobsters," said Mr. Ted. "I don't believe anybody can find it as fast as Miss Cherry and I can burn it up."

"We can!" cried Juggins and Joey together. And away they went again. They looked here and there among the rocks, and very soon they began to find the

pieces of driftwood that the ocean washes in at high tide. As soon as they had an armful of it, they ran back to the fire.

Before long more people began to come down the hill from the summer cottages, bringing baskets full of things to eat. Every time that Juggins came back with the wood, there were more piles of sandwiches and oranges and cookies. There was even a sack of peanuts, and after a while Madame Eliot's Katie came, bringing a large red tin box.

"It's sugared doughnuts," said Joey. "Granny's sent enough for everybody."

Juggins hoped that they would not have to get very much more wood. They had picked up all the pieces near the fire, and now they had walked along the shore as far as Mad Cap Island without finding anymore. Then Juggins had an idea. When the tide was high, there was a wide stretch of blue water between the rocks and the island, but now, at low tide, there was a little narrow strip of pebbles on which one could walk across the island.

"I know," said Juggins. "We can go over to Mad

Cap and hunt for wood. There'll be lots of it, because
nobody lives there."

So they tiptoed across on the narrow strip of wet
pebbles. The shore of Mad Cap was wild and rough,
and the rocks were too steep to catch much driftwood.
It was hard climbing, but Juggins and Joey scrambled
along as well as they could over the rocks. Soon they
went around a bend in the shore, and then they could
not see the lobster fire anymore. After a while they
came to a pebbly beach, and there at last were some fine
sticks of wood scattered about. Above the beach, among
the spruce trees, was an old tumble-down fisherman's
hut. Nobody lived in it, and its door was swinging loose
in the wind and creaking. Juggins and Joey began to feel
very far away indeed from the lobster roast.

They each picked up one of the sticks of wood and
began to scramble back along the shore as fast as they
could. It was harder than ever to climb over the rocks,
now that they had the wood to carry, and Juggins
thought that they would never come in sight of the
lobster roast again. But when at last they climbed
around the bend, there was the cheerful smoke from

the fire down the shore, and there were the bright sweaters of all the people sitting about it. They looked small and far away, but Juggins could see that they had begun to eat the lobster.

"Let's run," said Juggins, who was as hungry as she could be.

But when she and Joey looked down at the shore in front of them, there was no place to run to! Instead of the strip of pebbles, there was now a strip of blue water between the lobster roast and Juggins and Joey.

"Who put the ocean in there?" asked Joey, very much surprised.

"It's the tide," said Juggins. "We stayed too long. It's come in!" And they looked at each other with scared faces.

"When will it go out?" said Joey.

"In the middle of the night," said Juggins, who knew all about tides.

"But I shan't like it here in the middle of the night," said Joey, looking very sober.

"Perhaps they'll see us before that," said Juggins, "and take us off."

So they both stood up on a high rock and waved their arms and shouted as loud as they could. But they were too far away for anybody to hear, and the people at the lobster roast were all too busy eating to stop to look at Mad Cap Island. Far away down the shore, Juggins and Joey could see them pulling the lobster out of the seaweed and passing the baskets of goodies around and around. Very soon they would be all gone. And then Katie's red tin box gleamed in the sunshine. Everybody was eating doughnuts.

"They had extra sugar on them," said Joey, blinking a little.

"Oh, dear," said Juggins, blinking a little too. "What shall we do?"

Just then there was a shout. Mr. Ted had looked over at Mad Cap Island and was leaping across the rocks as if his fisherman's boots were seven-league boots instead.

"You young scalawags!" said Mr. Ted, as he walked right into the water, "we thought you had both run home for your suppers."

The water was not very deep, and in just a minute

Mr. Ted had carried Juggins and Joey safely over to the mainland. Then they all ran back across the rocks, and Miss Cherry and the others stood up and cheered and waved their paper napkins.

And there were plenty of good things left after all. Juggins and Joey sat on a rock beside Miss Cherry, with paper napkins tucked under their chins, and had all the lobsters and sandwiches and oranges and cookies that two little people could possibly eat. And then while they were eating their sugar doughnuts— but this belongs to the next chapter!

CHAPTER 7

WHO IS THE RED ROBBER?

WHILE JUGGINS AND Joey were eating their sugared
doughnuts, they climbed to the top of the little cliff at
the back of the flat rocks.

"We can see all the green islands from up here,"
said Juggins. "P'raps we'll see the Red Robber hiding
somewhere."

So they stood under the spruce trees at the edge
of the cliff and looked out to sea for the Red Robber.
They looked up and down the shore of every one of
the little green islands, but there was nothing moving
out there at all. Then suddenly something moved quite
close to them, and, for the first time, they saw that two
other bright eyes were looking out to sea. There on
the edge of the cliff, very small indeed in front of the

big ocean, sat Tansy, with his yellow tail curled around his toes.

"Oh," said Joey, "Granny never lets him go so far away from home."

"We'll take him back," said Juggins.

"Come kitty, kitty, kitty," said Juggins and Joey together, slapping their knees.

But Tansy had no idea of being taken anywhere, and if he could have talked, he would have told Joey that he came nearly every day by himself through the woods to sit on the cliff—though he never looked for the Red Robber.

Just as Juggins put out her hand to pick him up, Tansy took his tail from around his toes and slipped from under her hand. Then he ran off along the narrow little path at the edge of the cliff, his tail twitching in the air. Juggins ran after Tansy, and Joey ran after Juggins. When Juggins and Joey ran a little faster, Tansy ran a little faster too, and never once could Juggins get her fingers on more than just the tip of his fluffy tail. So they played "follow-your-leader" until the little path took them around the turn of the cliff into Back Cove.

Then just ahead of them, on a flat rock at the very edge of the cliff, they saw a cluster of freshly painted little lobster buoys, standing in the sun to dry. They had no faces or yellow jackets; they were just plain little lobster buoys with green stripes around them.

Tansy went frisking by the lobster buoys and into the woods, but Juggins stopped short, for there was a little house close by, and the path led right in front of it.

"It's Jem Bass's," whispered Juggins, standing behind a big rock that jutted out into the path and peeking around it. "I guess we'd better go back."

But before she and Joey had time to turn and run away, the door of the little house opened, and out came Jem Bass himself with another fisherman.

"Oh!" cried Juggins, right out loud—for there in Jem Bass's hand, swinging by her rope hair, was Geraldine!

Luckily, Jem Bass was so busy talking that he did not hear Juggins at all.

"Look here," said Jem Bass to the other fisherman, "if they really want to find out who's robbing the lobster traps, *I'll* tell 'em. Do you see this here lobster buoy?" Juggins and Joey, flattened against the other side of the rock, knew that Jem must be holding up Geraldine. "Well," went on Jem Bass, "I picked that up floating around out there in the fog the other morning, after the traps had been robbed, and it's Tom Tibbetts' lobster buoy. I tell you, he's the robber."

"Tom goes out in a dory still, doesn't he?" said the other fisherman.

"Sure," said Jem Bass, "and so does the man who robs the traps. Is there anybody else around here who hasn't got a motorboat?"

Jem's voice began to sound further away now. The

There in Jem Bass's hand was Geraldine.

men were walking along the path into the woods
where Tansy had gone. In a minute Juggins and Joey
could not hear them anymore. Then Juggins stood up
straight in the middle of the path. Her cheeks were
red, and her little brown hands were clenched tight.

"He's a *bad* man," she said, with a sob, looking at the
woods where the fisherman had disappeared.

"*I* don't believe your father's the Red Robber," said
Joey loyally.

Juggins stared at Joey.

"*Of course* my daddy isn't!" she said.

Then suddenly Juggins felt very bad and wicked
herself. She walked right across the path to the flat rock
where Jem Bass's freshly painted little lobster buoys
were drying in the sun, and with the toe of her sandal
she kicked them, one by one, off the edge of the cliff,
clattery-bang, down among the jagged rocks below.

Joey looked rather scared.

"Shall we go back to the lobster roast now?" he said.
Far away, on the rocks, they could hear the jolly sound
of people singing.

"No," said Juggins.

All at once Juggins just wanted to see Daddy. And she ran into the woods without even waiting to see if Joey was coming too. She ran without looking where she was going, stumbling over the roots of the trees in her hurry to get back to the little gray house.

So they thought Daddy was the Red Robber, said Juggins over and over to herself as she ran along—*her* daddy—because she and Daddy hadn't any motorboat and because Geraldine had been found floating. What would Daddy say when he heard it? But no, she shouldn't ever tell Daddy the dreadful thing that Jem Bass had said about him. And Joey mustn't tell either. Juggins looked behind her for Joey, but he was not there. He must have gone back to the lobster roast.

When Juggins came out on the road, she stopped running and wiped her eyes on the sleeve of her shirt. She did not like to have anybody, even Daddy, see her cry. A lamp was already shining cheerfully in the window of the little gray house, and when she opened the door, there was Daddy at the table, finishing his bread and tea just as if nothing at all had happened. Juggins began to feel better right away.

"Hello," said Daddy. "Does anybody want to row me across the harbor to get some bait?"

"Oh, yes," said Juggins, with a faint little smile.

She liked to row Daddy across the harbor, because when she did, they always played that he was a young man from the city who did not know anything about boats, and Juggins had to help him into the *Pea Pod* and tell him where to sit and push the boat off all by herself.

"Well then," said Daddy, with an extra little twinkle in his eyes, "go and get your sweater right away. It's nearly dark."

So Juggins ran into the bedroom and reached up to the hook in the corner behind the door, where the little old sweater always hung. The sweater wasn't there, but Juggins felt something else on the hook, and when she took it down, it was the blue-and-white-check zipper jacket from Mrs. Milly Willy's store!

"Is it really for me?" said Juggins, standing astonished in the kitchen door. Daddy nodded his head, and then Juggins was so glad that she couldn't think of anything to say.

74

When she had put on the new jacket and had zipped it up to the very top, she and Daddy went down to the float and got into the *Pea Pod*. Juggins told Daddy to be sure to sit right in the middle of the boat and not to drag his hands in the water. Then she put in her oars and rowed away across the harbor. The water was all pink with the sunset, and Daddy was a very funny young man from the city, so they had a very nice row indeed. By the time they came home with the bait, Juggins was feeling almost quite happy again.

As she sat on the edge of her little bed taking off her sandals, it began to seem to Juggins like a bad

dream that Jem Bass had said that dreadful thing
about Daddy. Then, just as she put on her little white
nightie, she thought of something. If they could only
find the real Red Robber, then Jem Bass would *know* it
was not Daddy.

They must begin tomorrow to hunt hard for the
Red Robber.

Then Juggins put the little blue-and-white-check
jacket on the chair beside her, where she could feel it if
she woke up in the night—which she never did—and
then she hopped into bed.

CHAPTER 8

WHAT THEY FOUND ON MAD CAP

THE NEXT MORNING when Juggins peeked out between the blue cotton curtains, she saw that it was misty in the harbor and that outside, by Mad Cap Island, the fog was very thick indeed. When Daddy said that it was too thick for them to go out to the lobster traps, Juggins looked very sober. It would be a wonderful day to hunt for the Red Robber.

As soon as breakfast was over, Daddy went out in front of the little gray house to make a new lobster trap. Juggins liked to hold the nails and measure the slats when Daddy made lobster traps, but this morning she put on her new zipper jacket and went to find Joey instead. She wanted to show Joey the jacket, and she must be sure that he did not tell anybody about the dreadful thing that Jem Bass had said about Daddy.

When she was halfway up the little path through
the pasture, she saw Joey coming down. He had on his
cork jacket again, and he seemed to be in a hurry.

"Look!" called Juggins, as Joey came running to
meet her. She stood in the middle of the path and
zipped the zipper up and down and smiled.

But Joey's mind was on something else, and he
hardly looked at the zipper jacket.

"Hello," he said. "Granny doesn't think your father's
the Red Robber. And Mr. Ted doesn't either, or Miss
Cherry."

"Do they all know about it?" said Juggins, her eyes
round with dismay.

"Oh, yes," said Joey, "I guess everybody knows it
now."

"Oh," cried Juggins, with a long breath, "then we
must find the Red Robber. We must find him right
away now." And she turned and ran down the little
path as fast as she could.

"Granny's going to do something," said Joey,
panting along behind. "Granny says she's going to

give a lot of money to anyone who finds the Red
Robber."

But Juggins hardly heard what Joey was saying. She
was thinking hard of what they could do to find the
Red Robber.

"I know," she said, when they came to the little gray
house, "we can row down the harbor in the *Pea Pod*
and wait at the edge of the fog. Sometimes it goes out
very quick, and if we are right there, perhaps we'll see
him before he can hide."

So Juggins and Joey ran down on the float and
began to untie the *Pea Pod*. While they were doing
it, Daddy looked up from his lobster trap, and then he
took his pipe out of his mouth.

"Where are you going?" asked Daddy.

"We're—we're going rowing," said Juggins.

Daddy looked out to sea, where the wind had driven
the fog to the very mouth of the harbor; then he
looked up at the sky. Daddy could always tell about the
weather by the wind and the sky.

"All right," he said. "Only be sure you don't row
beyond this end of Mad Cap."

Juggins and Joey got into the *Pea Pod* and pushed off from the float. Then Juggins put in the oars and began to row down the harbor. The *Pea Pod* was a wide little boat and quite flat, so it could not possibly tip over; but, unless you rowed quite well, it was hard to keep it from going around in a circle. Juggins was a good strong little rower, however, and the *Pea Pod*

went along very smoothly toward Mad Cap. There was not so much mist now, and the island could be clearly seen. Joey sat in the stern of the *Pea Pod* and watched Juggins dip the oars up and down. It looked very easy.

"I could do that," said Joey. "I want to row too."

"All right," said Juggins, "you can row one oar, and I'll row the other."

So Joey moved over on the seat with Juggins.

"I'll count," said Juggins, "and whenever I say a number, you must put your oar in."

Joey took tight hold of his oar with both hands.

"ONE," said Juggins—and, splash, came a shower of water all over the boat!

"TWO," said Juggins—and around went the *Pea Pod* in a circle!

"THREE," said Juggins—and up went Joey's oar into the air!

For Joey had caught a crab—not the kind of crab that you put in a salad, but the kind that makes you catch your oar in the water and go over backward into the bottom of the boat, with your legs waving around. Joey waved very fast for a minute because he couldn't get up in his cork jacket.

"Somebody hit me," said Joey in a very surprised voice, from the bottom of the boat.

Juggins put down her oar and pulled at the cork jacket. Then up came Joey, still looking very surprised.

"You can row now," said Joey. And he sat down in the stern seat again and held the sides of the *Pea Pod* with both hands.

After that Juggins rowed along very smoothly until they came to Mad Cap Island. Daddy had said that they must not row any farther than this, but the fog had drifted to the outer end of Mad Cap, and how could they look for the Red Robber in here?

"Let's land on Mad Cap," said Juggins. "There's a beach right there. Then we can walk to the end of the island where the fog is."

So Juggins rowed the *Pea Pod* up on a little pebbly beach, and they both jumped out. They tied the boat by its rope to a big stone. Then they started along the shore. There were not so many big rocks on this side of the island as there were on the other side, where they had been on the day before—just pebbles and small stones that did not have to be climbed. Once Juggins stopped and picked up some empty sea urchin shells, round dainty little cups that looked as if they had come out of a china shop.

"When Daddy and I have an ice cream cone," said

Juggins, "sometimes we put it in the sea urchin cups and play it's a party."

Juggins dropped the shells into the pockets of her zipper jacket, and they ran on until they came to the big rocks at the outer end of the island. Juggins and Joey climbed up to the top of the rocks and sat down. Just in front of them were the pounding surf and the open sea and the fog. It was very exciting, but they did not see the Red Robber.

"That rock's moving," said Joey suddenly, pointing to the shore below. "Something's going into the water."

Juggins looked.

"The seals!" she cried, jumping up. "They're the first this year. They almost always come to Mad Cap.

One—two—three—four—five—oh, they're sliding off! Sh! We mustn't talk."

Juggins put her hand over her mouth, but it was too late. At the sound of voices, the five little gray seals, just the color of the rocks, quickly slid off the wet seaweed into the water, and then all that Juggins and Joey could see of them were the five little round heads bobbing away from shore on top of the waves.

"Oh, dear," said Juggins, watching them swim away, "I *know* they won't come back."

"But there's another rock moving down there," said Joey.

Through a crack between two big rocks, they could certainly see something wriggling up and down. Very quietly, without saying a word, Juggins and Joey crept down and peeked over on the other side. There on the seaweed, its flipper caught in the crack of the rocks, was a very little seal. It was flopping about on the seaweed, trying to get free, and as soon as it saw Juggins and Joey, its big soft eyes grew wild with fright, and it flopped so hard that it almost tore its little flipper off.

84

"Oh, you poor little seal!" said Juggins. And she knelt down on the seaweed and put her arm about the slippery body. Then she twisted the flipper out from between the rocks as gently as she could.

"I'm going to take it home to show Daddy," said Juggins, standing up with the wriggling seal clasped tightly in her arms. "I guess I can hold the top of it, but you'll have to hold the tail."

So Joey took hold of the tail, and they started back over the rocks. As they went over the highest ones, they could look across the island to the deserted fisherman's hut. There was no breeze today, so the old door was not flapping, but just as Juggins and Joey looked at it, it was suddenly pushed open from the inside, and a man walked out. Juggins caught her breath.

"It's Jem Bass!" she said.

Juggins and Joey never knew how they got back to the *Pea Pod.* Not daring to look behind them, to see if Jem Bass was coming, they stumbled along over the loose stones of the beach, carrying the struggling little seal. It did not seem to be quite so

frightened now, but it was a very slippery little animal, and Juggins and Joey had to hold very tight to both ends. At last they came in sight of the *Pea Pod*. Then Juggins stopped short.

"There's another boat on the beach," she said. "What if it's Jem Bass's!"

But it wasn't. It was Mr. Ted's, and he and Miss Cherry were just coming around the end of a big rock.

As soon as Joey saw them, he was so glad that he dropped the tail of the little seal and ran to meet them. But as soon as he dropped the tail, the little animal began to slip, slip, slip through Juggins' arms.

"Oh, somebody come quick!" cried Juggins. And she stood still in the middle of the beach and held on as hard as she could.

Mr. Ted looked over at Juggins.

"What on earth!" he began. Then he ran quickly and caught the little seal just as its round head was slipping through Juggins' hands.

Then Juggins took hold of its tail, and together they put it safely at last into the bottom of the *Pea Pod*.

When Juggins and Joey had told Mr. Ted and Miss Cherry all about the seals, Mr. Ted pushed the *Pea Pod* into the water and helped Juggins and Joey to get in. Then he pushed them off, and he and Miss Cherry stood on the beach and waved, while Juggins rowed the *Pea Pod* up the harbor. There was no mist now, and the fog had gone far out to sea.

Suddenly Juggins looked very sober.

"We didn't see the Red Robber at all," she said. "We shall have to come again." Then she looked down at the bottom of the boat, where the little seal was flopping about from one side to the other, and smiled a little. "But we found *something*, anyway," she said.

"What shall we name it?" said Joey.

Juggins stopped rowing and leaned on her oars for a minute, while she thought of all the names she knew.

"We could call it Little Orphan Annie," she said.

And so they did.

CHAPTER 9

SEVERAL THINGS HAPPEN

LITTLE ORPHAN ANNIE spent the night in the bottom of the *Pea Pod*. The first thing the next morning, Juggins and Joey went fishing and caught six cunners for her breakfast. When they put the cunners into the *Pea Pod*, Little Orphan Annie gobbled them up right away, heads, tails, fins, and all. But still she did not seem quite happy. She sat at one side of the boat, her little round head just above the edge, and looked at the water. Whenever Juggins and Joey came near the *Pea Pod*, she flopped about so much that they were afraid she would flop right over the side of the boat.

"Perhaps she wants a drink," said Joey.

So Juggins brought a pan of nice cool water from the little green pump. Little Orphan Annie could not tell them that she did not like fresh water, but the next time she flopped, she flopped right into the pan and upset the water all over the inside of the boat.

"Never mind," said Juggins. "She likes sitting where it's wet anyway."

"We could bring her some seaweed to sit on," said Joey.

So Juggins and Joey ran down on the rocks at the edge of the harbor and brought armfuls of dripping brown seaweed to make a nice bed at one end of the boat. But poor Little Orphan Annie just flopped under a seat at the other end.

All day long Juggins and Joey trotted back and forth, trying to make Little Orphan Annie happy. They gathered rock snails and dug them out of the shells for her, but she turned away her little round head from the snails. They brought ever so many small stones and put them under the seaweed to make it look more like Mad Cap Island. Then they caught some more cunners. Late in the afternoon, Mr. Ted and Miss Cherry came with some of their friends to see Little Orphan Annie.

It was a very exciting day, and it was not until Joey had gone home and Juggins had said goodnight to Little Orphan Annie and come in for supper that she noticed Daddy's eyes. There was no twinkle in them at all. Juggins had never seen Daddy look just like that before. Could it be that he had heard about the dreadful thing that Jem Bass had said? Daddy never talked very much, but tonight he hardly said a word until they had finished their bread and tea. Then he said something so nice that Juggins forgot his eyes for a little while.

"Some of the lobster traps need to be mended," said Daddy. "Tomorrow we'll bring them in. And we'll bring in the lobster buoys, too, and paint them."

"Oh, goody!" said Juggins. It was fun having her lobster buoy children come home to be painted. She liked to help Daddy put them into new yellow jackets, and when they were all fresh and bright, she sometimes gave them a party.

The next morning Juggins got up very early so that she would have time to give Little Orphan Annie her breakfast and bring her fresh seaweed before Daddy was ready to go out in the dory. Little Orphan Annie did not flop quite so much this morning, and Juggins hoped that she was getting used to her new home. But she did look rather sad, and Juggins waved to her as she and Daddy rowed off down the harbor to get the lobster traps.

When they came back, they brought eight of the lobster buoy children with them. There was no fog again this morning and no Red Robber to be looked for. The ocean was sunny and blue, and Juggins could not help feeling happy as she rode home in the dory on top of the lobster traps with her smiling children all around her.

After dinner she and Daddy set the little lobster buoy children in a row on a bench outside the house. Then they went into the tiny shed, and Daddy passed the cans of paint down from the shelf to Juggins.

"There's lots of yellow," said Juggins, peeking into the cans, "but there's hardly any red. Shall we have to give the children blue grins?"

"We'll see," said Daddy.

Then they each took a brush and set to work. Daddy could paint faster than Juggins because his brush was ever so much bigger, but she did Tiny Tim and Mr. Hoover all herself. Daddy painted blue buttons on the front of his jackets, and they looked very fine, but Juggins just made a blue line up and down Tiny Tim and Mr. Hoover.

"They're zipper jackets," said Juggins.

When the lobster buoy children were all bright and shining in their new clothes, Daddy mixed a little turpentine with the red paint, and there was enough, after all, to give everybody a grin from ear to ear. Tiny Tim and Mr. Hoover grinned more than the others—but then, their jackets zipped.

After Daddy had put away the paints and gone down to his lobster traps on the float, Juggins stood in front of the lobster buoy children and thought about Geraldine. What had Jem Bass done with poor

Geraldine? Was she lying alone somewhere off on the rocks? Would she ever again have a bright yellow jacket and a happy red smile like the others? Juggins sighed a little as she thought of Geraldine.

Just then she saw Joey coming down the little path through the pasture. He was running as fast as he could in his cork jacket, and he was waving something white. Juggins ran out into the road.

"What's that?" she asked, looking at the envelope in Joey's hand.

"Granny's written something about the Red Robber.

I've got to take it to the constable's," said Joey, looking very important. "Can you come too?"

"To Amos Alley's?" asked Juggins. She had never in her life been to Amos Alley's door, except with Daddy.

"Yes," said Joey. "It's about catching the Red Robber. I guess they'll get him now."

"All right," said Juggins, "I'll go."

So she and Joey walked along the road, past all the fishermen's houses, until they came to the constable's. Amos Alley was not sitting on his porch today, so they tiptoed up the gravel walk and knocked softly at the kitchen door. Nobody came, so they knocked again. They had to knock four times before they heard heavy feet coming slowly toward the door. Then it was suddenly opened wide, and there stood Amos Alley himself, very tall and dark. He looked down at Juggins and Joey over his spectacles and grunted, but he did not speak.

"Hello," said Joey, looking up to the top of Amos Alley and not feeling quite so important, "Granny sent this." And he held out the envelope.

Amos Alley grunted again and took it.

"Goodbye," said Joey quickly, and he turned and ran away as fast as he could.

But Juggins did not move from the doorstep. She had not heard a word that Joey had said, and she was staring right past Amos Alley into his house. Standing on Amos Alley's kitchen shelf, beside the clock, was Geraldine!

In a moment the door had closed, and Juggins was running after Joey to tell him what she had seen. But although they talked about Geraldine all the way back to the pasture path, neither of them could think what she could possibly be doing in Amos Alley's kitchen.

When Juggins came to the little gray house, Daddy was leaning on a lobster sign, waiting for her. She stood beside him while six fishermen went by on their way home from Back Cove.

"Hello," said Daddy to the fishermen.

"Hello," said Juggins too, for she knew them all.

But the fishermen did not say *hello* or even notice Daddy and Juggins. They just strode along down the road as if there were nobody there. Juggins looked after them in astonishment. Then she looked up at Daddy's eyes. Then she knew. The fishermen all believed that Daddy—*her* daddy—was the Red Robber, and they would not speak to him anymore.

"Who's going to get supper?" asked Daddy.

Juggins ran fast into the little gray house. But when Daddy came into the kitchen, there was nobody putting the kettle on for tea or bringing the bread from the cupboard. For Juggins was on her little bed in the corner with her face in the patchwork quilt.

CHAPTER 10

LITTLE ORPHAN ANNIE GOES TO A PARTY

WHEN JUGGINS CAME out into the kitchen the next morning, Daddy was not there, but her bowl of cereal and cup of milk were waiting for her on the table. Daddy always left them there when he had to go away early. He must have thought of Little Orphan Annie, too, this morning, because there were three cunners in a pan on the doorstep. Before she ate her breakfast, Juggins took the cunners out of the pan and ran down the rocky little path to the float.

Little Orphan Annie did not flop at all this morning when Juggins climbed into the *Pea Pod*, and she ate her cunners right up, but her eyes seemed bigger and rounder than ever, and Juggins thought that she looked a little strange and lonesome sitting in the fog in the bottom of the *Pea Pod*. Juggins brought a handful of fresh seaweed with a crab in it for Little Orphan Annie. Then she went back to the kitchen and sat down to eat her cereal.

Juggins wondered where Daddy was. Perhaps he had gone to find Barney. She hoped that he would bring Barney back with him, for Barney was their best friend, and he would tell everybody that Daddy couldn't be the Red Robber. Juggins felt a little strange and lonesome, too, sitting there by herself in the little gray house with the fog outside. So she was very glad when she heard footsteps coming across the grass from the road. Perhaps it was Daddy with Barney. But then she heard a voice and knew that it was somebody else.

"Go home," said the voice, "*go home, GO HOME!*"

Juggins ran to the door, and there was Joey with a little tin pail in his hand. He was shaking the pail at Tansy, who was following behind.

"*GO HOME,*" said Joey again.

But Tansy, who always did exactly what he liked, had no idea of going home and scampered away through the grass after a cricket instead.

"Look," said Joey, holding out the pail to Juggins, "I picked them in Granny's garden. They're for you."

"Oh," said Juggins, looking in, "I *love* those."

The pail was almost full of bouncing big red raspberries. Joey looked at the kitchen table.

"Shall I put them in two saucers?" he said.

Then Juggins had an idea.

"No," she said, "we'll put them in the sea urchin cups and have a party! And the children can come if they're dry." And she ran outside to feel the jackets of the lobster buoy children.

Down the rocky little path, through the mist, she could see the *Pea Pod* rocking back and forth against the float.

"I wish Little Orphan Annie could come too," said Juggins, "I think she needs a party."

Then Joey had an idea.

"We could have the party down on the float," he said.

"Yes," said Juggins.

So Juggins and Joey carried the lobster buoy children, two by two, by their rope hair, down to the float and set them in a circle as near to the *Pea Pod* as possible. Then Juggins brought the little sea urchin cups and filled them with the raspberries. There were exactly eight, so they put one in front of each lobster buoy child. There was a big old lobster in a pail on the float, and Juggins thought that he should come to the party too. So she turned the pail upside down and put the lobster on top of it, between two of the lobster buoy children. Joey was not sure that he liked this new guest. He looked a little too much like Grandfather Lobster.

"There aren't any raspberries for him," said Joey.

"We can give him some fish bait," said Juggins. And she took a piece out of the dory and put it on top of the pail in front of the lobster.

Then she caught Tansy, who had come down on the float, and put him on another upturned pail with another piece of fish bait. Tansy took one sniff of the bait. Then he jumped off the pail and ran away from the party as fast as he could.

"I wish Little Orphan Annie could come up here too," said Joey. "She can't see very well from down there."

Juggins looked at Little Orphan Annie in the bottom of the *Pea Pod*. Then she looked at the float where Daddy's half-mended lobster traps lay scattered about.

"I know," said Juggins, "we can take her out and put her under a lobster trap. Then she can see everything."

So they picked out the biggest of the traps and dragged it over to the *Pea Pod*. Then Juggins got into the boat, and while Joey stood ready with the trap, she clasped Little Orphan Annie tight around the middle and lifted her—plop—out upon the float. Then down went the lobster trap over her, and there was Little Orphan Annie, looking out with frightened eyes through the slats of her cage.

Just as the party was about to begin, Juggins thought of something else. She ran up the rocky little path and into the house. When she came out again, she was carrying the red plaid sash of her Sunday dress.

"Little Orphan Annie ought to have something on for the party," said Juggins. And while Joey lifted up the lobster trap, she tied the sash under Little Orphan Annie's chin.

Then Joey brought another piece of fish bait and put it in the lobster trap, and the party really began. Juggins and Joey sat down in the circle and helped the lobster buoy children eat their raspberries out of the sea urchin cups, while Little Orphan Annie, who did not like being dressed up, flopped around under the lobster trap and behaved very badly indeed. But then, it was her first party.

The raspberries were almost eaten up when Joey suddenly pointed to the rocks along the shore.

She clasped Little Orphan Annie tight around the middle.

"Tansy's going into the ocean!" he cried.

There, sure enough, was Tansy at the very edge of the rocks, dabbling for something in the water with his paw.

Juggins and Joey jumped up and ran as fast as they could along the shore to the rescue. But Tansy did not want to be rescued, and as soon as he saw Juggins and Joey coming, he went bounding away over the slippery rocks. Tansy came fishing by himself nearly every day and was quite used to slippery rocks.

But Joey was not. And suddenly his feet went out from under him, and down he slid, over the wet seaweed, splash, right into the water in his cork jacket.

"Oh, oh!" cried Joey.

"Oh, oh, oh!" cried Juggins.

Joey did not go very far, for the water was not at all deep.

"But I don't float!" said Joey, holding tight to the seaweed.

"You can't," said Juggins. "You're standing up."

Then she took hold of Joey's hands and pulled him safely back on the rocks again. But Joey was very wet indeed, and he did not want any more party. So he ran away up the little path through the pasture to find Granny.

When Juggins, walking by herself, came around the corner of the little gray house, she heard a strange banging sound down on the float. Daddy, who was sitting on the doorstep, heard it too, and he and Juggins ran down the rocky little path to see what was the matter. Exciting things were going on at the party. Little Orphan Annie's lobster trap was jumping up and down on the float, and inside it, poor Little Orphan Annie, hung up by her necktie on a nail, was struggling to get free.

"Oh, *dear!*" cried Juggins.

She lifted up the lobster trap, and Daddy quickly untied Little Orphan Annie. He took off her necktie and put it in his pocket. Then Juggins held her tight to the float while Daddy felt her gently around the throat with his fingers. When they were sure that she was quite all right, Juggins pulled out the nail and put the trap over her again. Then she shook her finger at Little Orphan Annie.

"If you flop anymore," said Juggins through the slats, "I shall put you right to bed in the *Pea Pod*."

But when Little Orphan Annie's bedtime came that night, she did not go to bed in the *Pea Pod* at all.

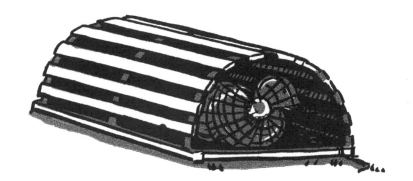

CHAPTER 11

SOMETHING IN A SHELL

DADDY DID NOT say a word all the time that he and Juggins were eating their dinner, and as soon as they had finished it, he went right away. Juggins sat down on the doorstep to wait for Joey, but Joey did not come. After a while she began to feel a little lonesome again. Then all at once she thought that she would go to see Mrs. Milly Willy, and she would take the overalls that Daddy had left on the chair because they needed a patch. Mrs. Milly Willy was always a very cheerful person to go to see, and she knew a great deal about patches. Juggins could sew on buttons nicely for Daddy, but sometimes her patches looked a little strange.

So she took the overalls and started off along the road that led to the end of the harbor. Perhaps,

thought Juggins, she might meet Barney or Mr. Ted
or somebody. But there was nobody to be seen on
the road or around the fishermen's cottages. When
she came to the constable's house, she wondered if
poor Geraldine was still standing up there beside
the kitchen clock. Amos Alley was not on his porch
today, but there was a white card stuck on the outside
of his gate with a thumbtack. Juggins stopped to see
what was printed on the card, and this is what she
read:

> ### $50 REWARD!
> WILL BE PAID TO THE PERSON
> WHO DISCOVERS AND IDENTIFIES THE
> ROBBER WHO IS STEALING LOBSTERS
> FROM THE BLUE HARBOR TRAPS
> (signed) ELIZABETH ELIOT
> AMOS ALLEY

Juggins was sure that this must be what Joey had
brought in the envelope to Amos Alley from his
granny. She spelled out the long words to herself
several times. She did not know what they all meant,
but Joey had said that his granny was going to give
a lot of money to catch the Red Robber, and the card
must be about that. Juggins stared at the figures at the
top and wondered how a person who had fifty dollars
would really feel. Everybody would try now to catch
the Red Robber. Perhaps they were all out looking for
him in the fog and would find him this very afternoon.
Then everyone would know right away that it wasn't
Daddy. Thinking about this, Juggins skipped along the
road to Mrs. Milly Willy's store.

There was nobody in the store except Muffin and
the kittens. The fluff balls had their eyes open now

and were crawling about the floor. Juggins patted them and told them that she would bring another cunner very soon. Then she looked through the door behind the counter that led into Mrs. Milly Willy's little kitchen, and there was Mrs. Milly Willy, in a fresh pink cotton dress, sitting at the table with her hooked rug. Even on foggy days, Mrs. Milly Willy's kitchen seemed full of sunshine, for there was a golden glow outside both the little windows, and two yellow canaries were always singing in their cages. Today Mrs. Milly Willy's shiny little tea kettle was singing away on the stove too. When it was damp, Mrs. Milly Willy always made herself a cup of afternoon tea. Juggins stood in the doorway, holding the overalls behind her.

"Hello," she said.

"Bless my soul!" said Mrs. Milly Willy, looking up with a smile all over her round, merry old face. "Whatever do *you* want in my store!"

"It begins with a *P*," said Juggins, smiling back at Mrs. Milly Willy. This was a game that Juggins and Mrs. Milly Willy played together very often.

"Potatoes," said Mrs. Milly Willy.

"No," said Juggins, shaking her head.

"Pumpkin pies," said Mrs. Milly Willy.

"No," said Juggins, shaking her head again.

"Prunes and pickled pigs feet," said Mrs. Milly Willy.

"No," said Juggins, shaking her head harder than ever.

"Give it up," said Mrs. Milly Willy.

Then Juggins held Daddy's overalls up in front of her, where Mrs. Milly Willy could see the big hole in the knee.

"Patch!" cried Mrs. Milly Willy.

"Yes," said Juggins.

Then they both laughed, and Mrs. Milly Willy got up from her chair and walked across the kitchen into the little closet where the ragbag hung. Juggins thought that Mrs. Milly Willy's ragbag must be very special, for whenever Mrs. Milly Willy put her hand into it, a piece of cloth just the right color always came out. In a moment Mrs. Milly Willy came back across the kitchen with a square of overall blue in her hand. Then Juggins sat down on a chair close by Mrs.

Milly Willy's and watched her set and baste the patch on the overalls with plump, deft fingers.

"Now you must sew it yourself," said Mrs. Milly Willy, "while I make my tea."

So Juggins took the overalls and Mrs. Milly Willy's thimble and, with the heels of her sandals on the rung of the chair, began to sew around the patch. She did not get on very fast because after every few stitches, Mrs. Milly Willy's big thimble dropped off her finger down upon the floor, and she had to stop and get it again. After a while, Mrs. Milly Willy sat down with her tea.

"Did you like to sew patches when you were a little girl?" asked Juggins, with a sigh, as she went after the thimble for the sixth time.

"No," said Mrs. Milly Willy, sipping her tea, "but I wasn't even five years old when I set my first patch."

"All by yourself?" said Juggins, astonished.

"Yes," said Mrs. Milly Willy, with a chuckle, "and I got sent to bed for it too."

"Why?" said Juggins, looking at Mrs. Milly Willy instead of at the patch. She never could remember to keep on sewing when Mrs. Milly Willy began to tell a story.

"Well," said Mrs. Milly Willy, "it was my old Aunt Dorcas who taught me to sew when I was a wee tiny child. She was very strict, and I was a willful young one, and I ran away from my sewing whenever I could. One day I heard Aunt tell my dad that if I lived to be a hundred, she was sure I'd not learn to mend his clothes for him because I would never sew all around a patch without running away.

"Now there wasn't anything I wouldn't do for my dad, small as I was. So that afternoon, when I found his old jeans on a chair with a hole in them, I thought I would show him that I could make a patch all by myself, in spite of Aunt. But I had nothing to make a patch with, and Aunt kept her ragbag locked up in her own closet, and I couldn't think where I could get any cloth. Then all at once I saw my apron strings and thought that Aunt wouldn't notice if one was a little shorter than the other. So I got the scissors and cut off a good piece at the end.

"My apron was pink, but I set the piece on Dad's jeans as straight as I could, and then I sewed it round and round and round until my little fingers were all pricked up. And funny enough it looked on Dad's old blue jeans, though I thought it was beautiful. But I forgot nobody could help seeing the patch, even if they didn't notice the apron strings! Aunt's sharp eyes were the very first to see it, and off I went to bed without my supper for spoiling my apron.

"But while I was lying there, crying in my little bed, up came Dad, secret-like, with a popover and a cookie for me in his pocket, and he told me he liked the patch, and if I'd be a good girl and mind Aunt, the next time he went to Boston in the schooner, he'd bring me something fine."

"Did he?" asked Juggins.

"Sure he did," said Mrs. Milly Willy. "And it was something so fine that after that, I could finish a patch without once putting it down."

"What was it?" asked Juggins.

Mrs. Milly Willy smiled at Juggins again all over her merry old face.

"It begins with *T*," said Mrs. Milly Willy.

"Tea set," said Juggins.

"No," said Mrs. Milly Willy.

Juggins wrinkled her forehead and thought, but she could not think of any other nice thing that began with a *T*.

"Give it up!" cried Juggins.

"Oh, oh," laughed Mrs. Milly Willy, shaking her finger at Juggins.

But she put down her cup of tea and walked over to the closet and took something out of a box on the shelf.

"If I let you look at it, will you finish your patch?" asked Mrs. Milly Willy.

"Oh, yes," said Juggins.

So Mrs. Milly Willy opened her hand, and there was

a funny little double shell with a hinge on one edge
and a hook on the other.

"But *shell* begins with an *S*," said Juggins.

"Look inside," said Mrs. Milly Willy, giving Juggins
the shell.

Juggins unfastened the little hook.

"Thimble!" she said. For there it was—a very small
silver thimble in a nest of red velvet. Juggins thought
it was prettier than anything she had ever seen.

"Shall I put it on, Mrs. Milly Willy?" asked Juggins.

"Sure," said Mrs. Milly Willy. And she went out into
the store to wait on a customer.

So Juggins put the little thimble on her finger, and
it fit as if it had been bought for her, instead of for
the little Milly who did not like to sew patches either.
Then Juggins picked up the overalls and began to
make stitches as fast as she could. And as the little
thimble did not drop off at all, she finished her patch
in a very few minutes.

When it was done, Juggins did not want to take
the little thimble off because it looked so nice on her
finger, but after a minute, she put it carefully away in

the shell and hooked the hook. Then she went out into the store where Mrs. Milly Willy was sitting behind the counter.

"Shall I put the thimble back on the shelf?" asked Juggins.

"No," said Mrs. Milly Willy.

So Juggins put it on the counter.

Then Mrs. Milly Willy took the overalls and looked at them. She seemed to like the patch, for she nodded her head and opened the glass case and took out a gumdrop, which she popped right into Juggins' mouth. Then she folded the overalls—and put the shell, little thimble and all, right into one of the pockets!

"We must push it way down in," said Mrs. Milly Willy, "so it won't fall out on your way home."

"Am I going to take it home?" asked Juggins, looking up at Mrs. Milly Willy with round, shining eyes.

"Sure," said Mrs. Milly Willy. "Now run along with you."

"Oh, thank you, Mrs. Milly Willy," said Juggins.

Then she ran, for she wanted to show the little thimble to Daddy as soon as ever she could.

CHAPTER 12

"IT LOOKS LIKE TOM"

AS SOON AS Juggins came out of Mrs. Milly Willy's store, she saw that there were some fishermen around Barney's new boat in the little open shed at the edge of the harbor. The mist was too thick for her to see who the fishermen were, but she thought that one of them was Daddy. So, holding tight the overalls and the precious thimble, she ran down over the grass to find him.

But when she came to the little shed and looked in, neither Daddy nor Barney was there. The other fishermen were walking around the boat, running their hands over its curving sides and rapping it here and there with their knuckles. One of them said that it was the finest boat he had ever seen.

The other fishermen were walking around the boat.

Juggins thought so too. It was all painted now, gleaming white, with a band of blue around the edge, and up in the prow, Barney had put a little carved white figure with its arms stretched out toward the sea.

"Oh," said Juggins under her breath when she saw it. She thought that it looked like a real little angel.

She tiptoed around behind the fishermen so that she could look at it closer, and then she saw something else. On the side of the boat, right under the little figure, Barney had painted the name:

JOLLY JOEY

Juggins caught her breath as she spelled out the words. Wouldn't Joey be happy! His own name on that wonderful boat! Juggins ran her fingers along the letters and reached up and touched the little white figure. Then she heard Barney's voice behind her, and when she turned, there was Daddy too. She was so glad to see him that this time she did not notice that none of the fishermen spoke to him, although they all said *hello* to Barney.

"Oh, Daddy," cried Juggins, running to him and

holding out the overalls, "see the patch I made for you, and see what Mrs. Milly Willy gave me!"

Juggins put her hand into the pocket of the overalls and felt around for the shell, but Mrs. Milly Willy had pushed it down very deep, and when Juggins finally pulled it out, she pulled out also the red plaid sash of her Sunday dress, which Daddy had stuffed into his pocket when he took it from Little Orphan Annie's neck. Juggins threw the sash over the edge of the boat and held out the shell to Daddy.

"Look," she began, "it opens like—"

And then she suddenly stopped. For Daddy was not looking at her or at the shell. He was looking straight at the fishermen on the other side of the boat, and the fishermen were all staring at her red sash.

For a moment nobody spoke, but Daddy and everybody else looked very strange. Juggins felt that something dreadful was going to happen, and she took hold of Daddy's hand. Then one of the fishermen shrugged his shoulders.

"It looks like Tom all right," he said, jerking his thumb at the red sash.

"Right out of his own pocket too," said another fisherman.

Juggins stared at the sash and at the fishermen. What did they mean? Then Barney, who was standing on the other side of Daddy, spoke.

"You boys are crazy," said Barney, bringing his fist down on the edge of the boat. "You ought to know that's the sash of a child's dress, not the Red Robber's scarf, and you ought to know that Tom Tibbetts would never touch a lobster that didn't belong to him."

"Oh, yeah?" said a third fisherman, shrugging his shoulders. "Well, that robber was seen out there this morning in the fog, and he had on a scarf just like that one." The fisherman pointed to the sash. "Did anybody see Tom around anywhere else early this morning?" he added. The other fishermen all shook their heads again.

"And Amos Alley has a lobster buoy over at his house now," said the first fisherman again, "that belongs to Tom. It was picked up floating the other day just where the traps had been robbed. Amos Alley has been keeping it till we should find out something else—and I guess we've found it now. Suppose you come along with us over to Amos', Tom."

Juggins, terribly frightened, had been looking from one to the other and holding tight to Daddy's hand. Suddenly she forgot to be afraid.

"That *is* my sash," she said, stamping her sandal on the floor of the shed and looking over the boat at the fishermen, "and my daddy *isn't* the Red Robber."

When she said this, Daddy looked down at her for the first time, but his face was not like Daddy's at all.

"Lucy Belle," he said, "I want you to run home now. I will come in a little while."

Then Juggins was more frightened than ever, for Daddy never called her *Lucy Belle* except when things were very solemn indeed. Long ago when she was little and had cut a new fish net with a knife, he had called her that, and also one other time, when they had gone to Portland to see old Great-Aunt Ann and she had not wanted to be kissed.

Juggins thought Daddy looked now exactly the way he had looked at Great-Aunt Ann's, so she walked very slowly out of the shed and across the grass. She

did not want to go away, back to the little gray house
alone, and leave Daddy with these cruel fishermen,
and her eyes were so blinky that she could hardly
see where she was going. Also, there was a dreadful
lump that she had to keep swallowing. But she walked
straight ahead and did not turn around until she came
to the road. She was afraid she might see them taking
Daddy to the constable's.

In front of Mrs. Milly Willy's, however, she wiped
her eyes on her sleeve and looked quickly back. The
men were still around the boat, and Barney was
standing close to Daddy. That made Juggins feel a

little better, but the lump was still there. As she ran
on, she did not see Mrs. Milly Willy out behind the
store feeding her ducks or Mr. Ted and Miss Cherry
waving to her from the pasture. She did not even
notice that she had left Daddy's overalls and the
precious shell behind her in the shed. It was hours
before she thought of her little thimble again because
of all the things that went on happening in this
strange afternoon.

The next thing happened when Juggins came to the
high place in the road just beyond Amos Alley's. The
fog was not quite so thick, and over the roofs of the
other fishermen's houses, she could see her own little
gray house and the float at the edge of the harbor. As
soon as she looked at the float, Juggins saw something
that made her stand still right in the middle of the
road. For Joey was down on the float in his cork jacket,
and he had just taken the big old lobster trap from
over Little Orphan Annie and was trying to lift her
back into the *Pea Pod.*

Now it was hard enough for two people to hold
Little Orphan Annie, but for one person, with a cork

jacket sticking out in front, it was impossible. Joey's fingers barely went around Little Orphan Annie, and Juggins, far away on the road, saw her begin to slip, slip, slip through his arms. Joey clutched and clutched, but it was of no use. Little Orphan Annie went right on slipping until she slipped—plop—right out of his arms and off the float into the water. In another moment she was swimming away, her little gray head bobbing on top of the harbor.

Juggins did not stop to see what Joey did next. She ran like mad down the hill and along the road to the little gray house. But when she came around the corner in sight of the float again, something *else* had happened!

CHAPTER 13

THE RED ROBBER AT LAST

JOEY HAD GONE after Little Orphan Annie in the *Pea Pod*! When Juggins came running down the rocky little path, he was already far out from the float, and he had lost one of the oars overboard. Juggins could still see Little Orphan Annie's round head swimming away into the fog, but Joey was not catching up with her at all. He was sitting in the middle of the sea, trying to row with one oar, and the *Pea Pod* was going around in a circle.

"Paddle back here," shouted Juggins.

"I can't," Joey shouted back. "The boat won't!"

Then Juggins saw that the *Pea Pod* was beginning to drift down the harbor. The tide was running out very fast, and although Joey kept on going around in circles, he went farther and farther away into the fog all the time. After a minute Juggins could only just see his one oar going up and down like the arm of a windmill.

"Oh, *dear!*" cried Juggins, clasping her hands.

What *should* she do? Somebody must go after Joey right away. But who? Juggins looked up at the road and along the shore. She could not see very far on account of the fog, but there was not a person in sight, and she knew that Daddy and Barney were far away. Then she looked at the dory. She had never in her life been out in it all alone by herself because Daddy said that it was much too heavy for her to row. By this time Joey and the *Pea Pod* had drifted so far into the fog that she could hardly see them at all.

Juggins ran over to the dory and began to untie it as fast as she could. The big rope was heavy and wet, and it seemed as if the knot never would come loose. But at last it did, and Juggins jumped into the dory and pushed it away from the float. Luckily Daddy had left the oars, and in a minute Juggins was standing up in the middle, just the way Daddy did, and rowing slowly out into the harbor. The oars were big and hard to lift,

but she remembered what Daddy had said about all the
Tibbettses having fine strong muscles in their arms
to row with, and she pushed and pushed, although her
face grew hotter and her breath shorter with every
push.

"Joey," she shouted between strokes, "where are you?
I'm coming in the dory." And somewhere in the fog,
she could just hear Joey calling:

"I'm over here."

Soon Juggins had rowed so far out into the harbor
that the dory began to drift with the tide, too, and they
went much faster. Then suddenly through the mist,
she saw the outline of the *Pea Pod*, with Joey still
splashing the oar up and down.

In a minute the dory and the *Pea Pod* were side by side.

"You must get in here," said Juggins. And leaning over, she held the two boats together, while Joey scrambled into the dory. Then Juggins took the rope of the *Pea Pod* and tied it to one end of the dory so that they could tow it home.

"Where's Little Orphan Annie?" said Joey, as soon as he was safely in the big boat.

Juggins and Joey stood in the middle of the dory and looked all around in the circle of fog, but as far as they could see, there was no little gray head swimming on the water.

"I think she went that way," said Joey, pointing.

"We can't go out any farther in the fog," said Juggins. "It's coming in thicker than ever. I guess we'll have to go home."

She looked very sober, for she did want to find Little Orphan Annie, but she was a good fisherman, and she knew the danger of going into the fog. So she picked up the big oars again and began to row for the float. It was harder than ever now because she had to row against the tide. Juggins pushed and pushed at the oars, while Joey sat on the opposite seat and looked back over the water for Little Orphan Annie.

"Your face is awf'ly red," said Joey after a few minutes.

Juggins dropped one of the oars and wiped her forehead, but when she stopped rowing, she heard a sound that made her look more sober than ever. It was the sound of waves off at one side, breaking on the rocks, and Juggins knew that they must be the rocks of Mad Cap Island. The dory had drifted to the very mouth of the harbor, and the strong tide was carrying them out to sea faster than she could row the boat home. Now that she was not rowing, Juggins could see how swiftly the tide was running, and the dory with it. She knew that that was how Mad Cap got its name— the tide rushed so madly by the island on its way out.

Quickly Juggins picked up the oars again and pushed with all her might. Her face grew hotter and redder than ever, as she tried to force the heavy dory against the tide. She could not see the shore because of the fog, so she was not sure whether they were going

ahead, but after a little while, she knew that they were
not, for she could hear the waves breaking now back
where they had come from, instead of off at one side.
The dory had drifted right out into the open ocean,
beyond Mad Cap Island.

"When are we going to get home?" said Joey, holding
to the sides of the dory, for the sea was rougher now.

"I don't know," said Juggins, her heart beating fast
as she struggled with the oars.

She had given up trying to row the dory ahead. All
she could do now was to keep it pointed into the waves
so that the water should not come over the side of
the boat. Juggins was used to being out on the ocean,

and she was not very much afraid, except for the fog. Perhaps some fishermen would come along soon and pick them up. If only the fog would go out, somebody would be sure to see them right away. She listened for the sound of a motor somewhere in the mist, but she could not hear any. Perhaps when the tide turned, she could row in herself. Juggins hoped that it would turn before they had drifted too far, for her arms were tired, and it *was* a little scary out there alone with Joey in the fog. Just then she saw a little yellow spot on the top of a wave, and then another and another.

"Oh, look," she said. For there were her own lobster buoy children dancing merrily on top of the water! It did not seem to Juggins half so far away from home now, with the family all around. But Joey did not look at the lobster buoy children. He suddenly stood up in the middle of the dory.

"There's somebody," he said, pointing ahead.

Juggins turned, and there indeed was a boat, quite close to them in the mist. It was another dory, and the fisherman in it was just leaning over to take in a lobster trap.

"He's pulling one of *our* traps!" whispered Juggins, astonished.

Sure enough, on the end of the rope that he was pulling was a lobster buoy with a bright yellow jacket and a grin. At that moment the fisherman stood up straight in his dory, with the lobster trap in his arms, and Juggins and Joey both squealed right out loud— for around the fisherman's neck, and up to his very ears, was a bright red scarf!

IT WAS THE RED ROBBER!

At the sound of the squeals behind him, the fisherman dropped the lobster trap back into the water with a splash and quickly reached for his oars, without once looking to see who was behind him. But just for a moment Juggins and Joey saw the face within the scarf. And when they saw it, they squealed again—for at last they knew just who the Red Robber was!

CHAPTER 14

ADRIFT

THE FACE THAT they saw in the red scarf was the
squinty, scowly face of Jem Bass.

Jem Bass was the Red Robber!

Juggins and Joey were so surprised that for a
moment they almost forgot where they were. But
when the other dory began to move away quickly into
the mist, Juggins felt all at once much more afraid of
the fog than of the Red Robber.

"Jem Bass," she called as loud as she could, "we can't
row in. Oh, Jem, won't you *please* take us home?"

But the Red Robber was gone. He had slipped
silently away into the mist without once looking
around. Juggins began to row as hard as she could
toward the spot where the other dory had disappeared.

"Oh, Jem," she cried again, with a little sob, "come back. Oh, *please* come back!"

When Joey saw that Juggins was really frightened, he began to be frightened too.

"I—I want to go home," said Joey, looking very white and little in the middle of the big sea. "I want to go home *now*."

"We can't," said Juggins, "but my daddy will come and get us. We must listen hard for the motorboat."

"Your daddy hasn't got a motorboat," said Joey.

"No," said Juggins, "but I *know* my daddy will come."

So they listened as hard as they could. Once they heard gulls screaming overhead, and once there was a bang that made them both jump, but it was only the *Pea Pod* that had been bumped against the dory by a heavy wave.

It was getting much rougher, and Juggins had all she could do to stand up in the middle of the boat. The dory went up and down, and up and down, and up and down, and every minute it was harder to keep it pointed into the waves with the heavy oars. But Juggins knew that she must. Good fishermen always stood by their oars, and Daddy had said that she was a good fisherman.

So they went on and on over the waves. Juggins did not know where they were or how fast they were drifting. It seemed to her that she and Joey were the only people in the world—a strange little round world, shut in by gray walls of mist and with a waving floor. All at once Juggins thought of something dreadful. What if they should drift out and out, beyond the green islands and out of sight of land, where Daddy could not find them at all? When she thought of this, Juggins began to push the oars again. But after a minute she stopped. Perhaps she was just rowing them farther out to sea.

It was darker, and the fog all around looked thicker. After a while it began to rain. Juggins held the oars with one hand, then reached down and pulled the slickers and sou'westers out from under the seat. She put on hers, and Joey put on Daddy's. The rain splashed down into Juggins' face and ran in little streams from the brim of her sou'wester so that she could hardly see the waves ahead. It ran in streams from Joey's, too, right into his lap, as he slid about on the wet seat. Joey's face looked smaller and whiter than ever with Daddy's big sou'wester pulled down over his ears. Before long he slid right off the seat into the bottom of the boat, in a miserable wet little heap.

"Oh, dear, oh, dear," sobbed Juggins. She did hope that Daddy would come very soon.

Just then, above the rain and the waves, there was a faint clanging sound from somewhere out in the fog. When Juggins heard it, she stopped sobbing and listened. She knew that it was the sound of the little black bell buoy that she could hear at night when she was at home in her own little bed. After all, then, they were not away out beyond the green islands where Daddy could not find them, but not very far from Mad Cap!

With a glad little catch of her breath, Juggins shook the water from her sou'wester and began to row toward the sound of the bell. Her arms did not feel half so tired now that she knew where they were. Sometimes the bell seemed to be on one side of them, and sometimes it seemed to be on the other, but after a while the sound came nearer, and then all at once there was the bell buoy itself, just ahead of them in the fog, rising and falling with the waves, like a tall black spider on top of the water.

As the dory slid by the bell buoy, Juggins dropped the oars and caught one of the iron legs with both her hands. It was like finding an old friend in the middle of the lonesome ocean.

"We must stay here with it, Joey," said Juggins, clinging to the bell buoy over the side of the dory. "Then we shan't be lost anymore."

But Joey did not even look up. He was sitting in the bottom of the boat, crying softly to himself, with his face in the sleeves of Daddy's slicker.

The dory and the bell buoy went up and down, and up and down. They banked against each other, and Juggins felt as if her arms were going to be jerked out, but she did not let go. After a while the sharp little barnacles all over the bell buoy began to cut into her hands. Then all at once she thought of something. She could tie the dory to the bell buoy.

"Joey," said Juggins, "you must get the rope. I can't let go."

The dory and the bell buoy went up and down.

So Joey lifted his head from the sleeves of the slicker and crawled along until he could reach the rope and hand it to Juggins. He did not feel half so much like crying now that he was helping. Juggins tied the rope to the leg of the bell buoy with a good square knot. When she was very little, Daddy had shown her all about tying boats. Then she and Joey sat down on the seat, and the dory and the bell buoy went up and down, and up and down in the rough sea, but Juggins felt ever so much safer. Daddy must be out hunting for them now. If only she could let him know that they were there.

Then Juggins thought of something else. She picked up an oar and struck the handle of it—bang—against the bell. It made a strange loud sound. She struck again, and over and over, bang, bang, bang-bang-bang.

"I want to do that," said Joey.

So Joey took the other oar and struck the bell too—bang, bang, bang-bang-bang—bang, bang, bang-bang-bang. Together they made a very loud noise indeed. Sometimes Joey struck other things besides the bell.

He struck the side of the dory, he struck the brim of Juggins' sou'wester so that it flew off into the water, and finally he struck his own hand on the edge of the boat.

"Ouch!" screamed Joey.

Then, for a little while, there was such a loud noise that neither Juggins nor Joey heard the chug-chug of a motorboat until it came out of the fog in front of them.

"Oh, Daddy, Daddy!" cried Juggins, dropping the oar, and holding out both arms.

For standing up in the motorboat, tall and grave, were Daddy and Barney.

"We caught the Red Robber," shouted Joey, before Barney had time even to stop his engine.

"Yes," shouted Juggins, "and it's Jem Bass!"

And Daddy and Barney looked as if they couldn't believe their ears!

In a moment they were close to the dory, and Daddy had lifted Juggins and Joey over the side of the motorboat. Then as soon as Barney had tied the dory and the *Pea Pod* on behind, off they went, chug-chug-chugging for the harbor.

Juggins and Joey sat close on either side of Daddy and told about everything that had happened, and before they had finished, Juggins noticed that Daddy's eyes were quite all right again. The twinkle had come back.

"Did my banging make a grand loud noise?" said Juggins.

Daddy nodded his head and pinched her cheek, as he always did when he was very much pleased.

"I made a noise too," said Joey.

"Sure you did," said Daddy, and he pinched Joey's cheek too.

It had stopped raining, and the fog was lifting when they came into the harbor. As they went by Mad Cap Island, some seals slipped off the rocks into the water, and Juggins could see that one of them was much smaller than the others.

"Oh, dear," she cried, sitting up very straight. "It's Little Orphan Annie, and I want her!"

"Don't you want to go home?" asked Daddy.

"Oh, yes," said Juggins.

"Well, perhaps Little Orphan Annie did too," said

Daddy. "Home's a good place."

Juggins looked up the harbor. The clouds were sailing away, and the windows of the little gray house gleamed at her in the sunset, like two bright, cheerful eyes. Then she looked back at Mad Cap.

"I guess I'll let Little Orphan Annie go home," said Juggins.

CHAPTER 15

THE BOAT IS LAUNCHED

THE NEXT DAY was very exciting. It seemed to Juggins that nearly everybody in Blue Harbor came to the little gray house. First of all, early in the morning, Barney came to say that Jem Bass had run away and that nobody knew where he had gone. The whole village was hunting for the place where he must have hidden his stolen lobsters, said Barney.

Then other fishermen came, and some of them were the same ones who had been in Barney's shed the day before, and they slapped Daddy on the shoulder and said that they were very glad indeed that he was not the Red Robber. One of them patted Juggins on the head and told Daddy that he ought to be proud to have such a fine little seaman, and Daddy smiled at Juggins and said that he was. That made her very happy, though she turned away her head.

Late in the afternoon, Madame Eliot stopped in her car on the way home from her drive. She had Mr. Ted and Miss Cherry with her, and they all shook hands with Daddy and said that Juggins was the bravest little girl in Blue Harbor. Then they carried her away with them to have supper with Joey.

Last of all, at bedtime Barney came again, to tell Juggins and Daddy that the new motorboat would be launched the next afternoon, and he brought with him the little thimble in a shell which Juggins had left in the shed. So *that* was all right. There would be exciting things tomorrow too, thought Juggins as she hopped into bed. But she did not guess at all *how* exciting they would be.

They began the very first thing in the morning. Before she opened her eyes, she could feel something heavy on her toes, and when she sat up and looked—there on top of the patchwork quilt was Geraldine! She had come home at last. Juggins held her favorite child at arms' length and looked her all over.

Geraldine's yellow jacket was peeling, and her rope hair was frayed, but her grin was still there, and her saucy little nose. Juggins gave Geraldine a real hug. Then she put her on the chair, and jumped out of bed,

and began to dress as fast as she could, for she had slept late, and the sun was high. Geraldine sat on the chair and looked very happy to be home.

Juggins put on a clean shirt and overalls for launching day and her zipper jacket, for the wind coming in through the window was cool. It was a fresh northwest wind that had blown every bit of the fog away, and the sea and the sky were sparkling at last.

"You shall have a new zipper jacket too, like Mr. Hoover," said Juggins to Geraldine, as they both went into the kitchen.

Daddy was not there, but the cereal was waiting on the table, and this morning Juggins did not feel lonesome a bit, with Geraldine sitting beside her on the chair. Before she had finished her cereal, there was the sound of scampering across the grass, and there was Joey at the door, so excited and out of breath that he could hardly speak.

"They've found heaps and heaps of lobsters hidden on Mad Cap," cried Joey, "and the red scarf in the little hut over there, and they've found Jem Bass's old dory tied somewhere—and—and everything—and Granny's going to give you the fifty dollars because you found the Red Robber, so now you can have your roof mended."

"You found the Red Robber too," said Juggins, when Joey stopped for breath.

"Yes," said Joey, "but our roof doesn't leak, so Granny and I think you better have it."

Juggins stared at Joey with round eyes. She could

not take in so many strange things all at once. She was still staring when Daddy and Barney came in through the door. Daddy took a piece of paper out of his pocket, and his smile was almost as wide as Geraldine's.

"That's it!" said Joey, "That's the check for the roof. I saw Granny write it. It's like money."

Juggins ran to look, and there, sure enough, on the bit of paper were the words: "Fifty . . . Dollars."

"Well, what do you think of *this* for the person who found the Red Robber?" asked Daddy, pinching her cheek.

Juggins took the check and looked at it. She did not feel at all the way she had thought she would if she had fifty dollars. She was thinking about the nice game with the pans that she and Daddy had always played when it rained.

"Can't we leave just two *teeny-weeny* little holes in the roof?" said Juggins to Daddy.

Then Barney took something out of his pocket. Nice things always came out of Barney's pockets, and this time it was a piece of blue ribbon made of real silk. Mrs. Milly Willy had sent it for Juggins to tie in her hair when she went to the launching. Juggins did not often have a real silk ribbon, and it made her almost as happy as the fifty dollars. She climbed on a chair in front of the kitchen mirror and took off the old piece of blue cotton that tied up her yellow topknot. Then she tied on the silk ribbon instead, and she made a nice square knot so that it would be sure not to come off.

"Oh, dear," sighed Juggins, looking at the ribbon in the glass, "I wish the launching were right away."

But the afternoon came at last, and she and Daddy started along the road to the end of the harbor. Ever so many other people were going too. Juggins could see them coming down the path from the summer cottages and trudging along the shore from the fishermen's houses.

When they reached Barney's shed, there were a lot more people around the boat. They were all dressed in bright summer clothes, and Juggins thought that it looked like a real party. Mr. Ted and Miss Cherry were there, and Mrs. Milly Willy, and Madame Eliot in her shimmery gray dress, holding Joey by the hand. As soon as Joey saw Juggins, he came running to meet her.

"Hello," said Joey in an excited voice. Then he stood right in front of Juggins, looking as if he could not think of anything more to say. He looked exactly as if he knew a secret that he must not tell!

"Come here, Joey," said Madame Eliot, and Joey ran back to his Granny.

Then Juggins and Daddy went into the shed and

stood beside Barney, close by the boat. It looked more beautiful than ever today, gleaming white in the sunshine. There was a spray of blue flowers from Madame Eliot's garden on the bow, under the little angel figure, and Madame Eliot's blue scarf was thrown across the boat so that nobody could see the name until it was time for the launching. Juggins looked across at Joey and wondered if he knew what was painted there and if he would be happy and surprised. Juggins held her breath and waited, very still, beside Daddy.

After a few minutes, when everybody was gathered around the boat, Juggins saw Madame Eliot nod her head at Mr. Ted. Then Mr. Ted stepped up close to the boat, and everybody stopped talking.

"I know we are all glad to be here," said Mr. Ted, "to see this beautiful boat go into the water. We hope she will bring the best of luck to her owner, for her owner is a fine, brave little fisherman. Madame Eliot has had the owner's name painted on the boat, and I am going to ask Lucy Belle Tibbetts here to pull off this scarf and read the name for us."

"Oh," said Juggins, drawing back a little against Daddy, her face pink, for everybody was looking at her and smiling.

But Mr. Ted held out his hand, and Juggins, her heart beating fast, went up to the boat and took hold of the scarf.

"Be sure you say the name loudly so that we all can hear," said Mr. Ted, in a laughing whisper.

"Yes," Juggins whispered back—and quickly pulled the scarf.

Then for a moment there was not a sound in the shed. Everybody was still looking at Juggins, and Juggins was looking at what was painted on the boat. Her mouth was wide open, ready to speak, and her eyes were even wider than her mouth. But Juggins could not say a word, for *Jolly Joey* was no longer there. Painted on the boat instead was the name:

LUCY BELLE

Then all at once the silence was broken by Joey's shrill little voice. Joey could not keep his secret any longer.

"The boat's for you!" cried Joey, dropping Madame

Eliot's hand and running over to Juggins. "From Granny and me, because you went after me in the dory! Aren't you glad?" said Joey, for Juggins stood still without moving, her eyes on the boat.

"Oh, yes," said Juggins under her breath, and she looked at Madame Eliot with a funny little trembly smile.

Then Mr. Ted picked Juggins up and set her right on the bow of her boat.

"Three cheers for Captain Tibbetts!" cried Mr. Ted, and they all cheered and waved their handkerchiefs at Juggins, who felt as if she must be in a dream.

When Mr. Ted had lifted her down again, Barney and the other fishermen put their shoulders against the boat and pushed and heaved, and in a minute the *Lucy Belle* was sliding down the little runway. Would she float? Juggins stood between Daddy and Mr. Ted at the very edge of the shed, her hands clasped tight.

Into the water, straight and smooth, went the *Lucy Belle*, and there she floated like a beautiful white swan, the little figure on the bow spreading its arms to the sea. Then everybody cheered again.

"Now we can go to the green islands and way out to sea—and everywhere," shouted Joey, capering around so near the edge of the shed that he almost fell off into the water.

"Hi there, you young scalawag," said Mr. Ted, catching Joey just in time. "Who's captain of that motorboat anyway?"

Juggins looked at Mr. Ted.

"My daddy is," she said, with a happy smile. And she put her hand in Daddy's.